Volume Eight

Insight Publishing Company
Sevierville, Tennessee

Volume Eight

© 2004 by Insight Publishing Company.

All rights reserved. No part of this book may be reproduced in any form or by any means without prior written permission from the publisher except for brief quotations embodied in critical essay, article, or review. These articles and/or reviews must state the correct title and contributing author of this book by name.

Published by Insight Publishing Company
P.O. Box 4189
Sevierville, Tennessee 37864

Printed in the United States of America

ISBN: 1-885640-54-4

Contents

A Message from the Publisher vii

Chapter 1
Dr. Warren Bennis 1

Chapter 2
Jack Lannom 13

Chapter 3
Terry Paulson, Ph.D 29

Chapter 4
Sam Allman 47

Chapter 5
Peter Quinones 67

Chapter 6
Les Brown 81

Chapter 7
Gregory J. Maciolek 93

Chapter 8
Maureen G. Mulvaney, CSP 111

Chapter 9
Christine Holton Cashen 125

Chapter 10
Ted Garrison 143

Chapter 11
Thomas Winninger 153

Chapter 12
Donald L. Rheem 175

A Message from the Publisher

"Two heads are better than one." If this time-tested saying is really true, then why not add more heads? Some say that too many cooks can spoil the broth, but when it comes to collecting wisdom about how to succeed in life, you really can't get too much advice, especially from those whose lives bear clear evidence that their strategies work!

If you are like most people, you may find it hard to digest and implement the lessons of a dozen books from a dozen unique authors. Wouldn't it be great to simply sit down and chat with a group of leaders who have proven that anyone can overcome life's obstacles and to hear the simple, unadulterated truths behind their life lessons? Now you can.

Mission Possible! should be required reading from anyone wanting to grow and succeed. Regardless of which life area you are trying to impact, these twelve personalities offer hope, encouragement, and practical advice that really works! You will feel as if they are all talking right to you, giving you a leg up on the competition and a pat one the back to help you succeed.

Don't miss a chapter of this exciting edition of *Mission Possible!*, and watch for new releases coming soon to a bookstore near you.

Interviews By David E. Wright
President,
International Speakers Network

Architect of one of the most successful business conglomerates in America and long-time speaker, trainer and business consultant, David Wright knows how to cut through the clutter and get to the heart of success in the speaking industry. David has worked exclusively with professional speakers, trainers and consultants since 1989, helping them implement innovative, hard-hitting marketing and public relations programs that have led to their success.

Chapter 1

DR. WARREN BENNIS

Warren Bennis has written or edited twenty-seven books, including the best-selling Leaders *and* On Becoming A Leader, *both of which have been translated into twenty-one languages. He has served on four U.S. presidential advisory boards and has consulted for many Fortune 500 companies, including General Electric, Ford and Starbucks.* The Wall Street Journal *named him one of the top ten speakers on management in 1993 and 1996, and* Forbes *magazine referred to him as "the dean of leadership gurus."*

The Interview

David E. Wright (Wright)
It is my sincere pleasure to be speaking with Dr. Warren G. Bennis. Dr. Bennis is a distinguished professor of business administration and founding chairman of the Leadership Institute at the University of Southern California. He also serves as chairman of the advisory board for the Center for Public Leadership at Harvard University's John F. Kennedy School of Government, and he is the Thomas S. Murphy Distinguished Research Fellow at the Harvard Business School. In addition to his books, Dr. Bennis has written more than 2,000 articles, which have appeared in the *Harvest Business Review, Fast Company* magazine, *The New York Times, Esquire, Atlantic*

Monthly, The Wall Street Journal, Psychology Today and numerous management-related publications. Dr. Bennis, it's an honor to talk with you today.

Dr. Warren Bennis (Bennis)

Thank you, David.

Wright

I don't know how comfortable you are with labels like genius, guru and legend, but it is a fact that many of our listeners consider you such. However, in the rare event that one of our readers is meeting you for the first time, would you offer us a brief overview of the high points of your life and career? In other words, how did your life's path bring you to this place?

Bennis

It's always difficult to answer those questions, because as you look back, you try to look for a pattern. I think, in my case, there were many eccentric precursors that led to where I am today. Being in the army in World War II was certainly a significant experience as was leading a platoon of infantrymen in Germany when I was nineteen. One of the men in my platoon used to talk about a college that he wanted to go to—Antioch College in Yellow Springs, Ohio. I had never heard of the college or the town, but I wound up going there because they had a co-op program in which you worked part of the year and went to school part of the year. That was my introduction to the idea of how you can bridge and yoke together theory and practice. You were in a classroom for twelve weeks, then working for twelve weeks, and then you returned to campus. You were always on a tightrope between the world of practice and the world of theory, research and intellectual inquiry. That was one of the reasons why college was such a profound experience; I learned that there was nothing as practical as a good theory. The other reason was that the college's president, Dr. Douglas McGregor, was the founder of the field of organizational behavior and leadership back in the '40s. He was my role model.

After college, I went to MIT, where I founded a group that was very serious about the field of leadership and organization. We started a department there, which was probably one of the first of its kind in the country, if not the world. I took my work/study idea seriously, and after being an academic for about twenty years, I decided to become a university president, which I did for about seven years. I ended up teaching, writing and consulting at the University of Southern California. That's roughly how I got from there to here.

Wright

Dr. Bennis, I spent some time this week on Amazon.com just scrolling through all the titles you've authored, co-authored or edited. It's a staggering collection. Of all the books that you've written, are there any that stand out in your mind as life markers for you or books that changed your life in significant ways?

Bennis

I don't know if they changed my life, but if I could be bold and audacious, I hope they've been able to change other people's lives somewhat. I think there are two or three books that I would like to underscore. My first book, *The Planning of Change*, was co-edited and co-authored with two of my mentors, Ken Benne and Bob Chin. It was a book of readings we compiled and long essays that we wrote, and I'm very proud of it, because it laid some of the groundwork for organizational and institutional change. It was published in 1961, at a time when there was not much literature on the subject, so I'm proud of that book. Another title I would mention, *On Becoming a Leader*, is the one that I enjoyed writing most, and it's the one that I life assign to my students, whether they're executives, high school students or undergraduates. It has been recently revised and is my personal statement about leadership. Finally, the book that I co-authored with Bob Thomas, *Geeks and Geezers*, has been recently published. It is about leaders age thirty-two and younger and leaders age seventy and older, and it compares the effects that two different eras have had on leadership. In my case, I'm a "geezer," and the most influential events in my experience were the Depression and World War II.

We compared a group with that background to the "geeks" group, who were born in the late '60s and '70s, and studied how those two groups differed. In the course of writing that book, we learned a great deal about how leaders develop, how people extract wisdom from experience and how people continue to grow despite their age.

Wright

Geeks and Geezers is one of the most unique titles I've ever read. At first glance, I thought, "Boy, this is not worthy of Bennis!" Then I read the subtitle, which adds significant context to the title: *How Era, Values and Defining Moments Shape Leaders*. It's a fascinating book. What led you to write it, and where did the idea come from?

Bennis

Two factors triggered the idea. First, I was interested in the generation that's grown up in the last twenty years or so. Right now, they're between the ages of twenty-two and thirty-two. In this country, there are more than eighty million people in that particular group. That's a bigger spike in population than we saw with the Baby Boomer generation. This is a group that's grown up "virtual, digital and visual." Many of these people had computers when they were in the first grade or kindergarten. That has to have affected the way they look at the world. They've grown up during a period of uninterrupted prosperity and in a time of options. They've also grown up in a time of U.S. hegemony. There's no question that we are now the single power in the world, far beyond what England was in the nineteenth century, when it ruled the waves. So I was interested in trying to understand this generation—their minds, their thoughts, their philosophies.

I was also interested in geezers, people like me, seventy years and older, who keep reinventing themselves, who keep their eyebrows raised in curiosity, who keep doing things that are exciting and interesting. Why do they do that, and what can we learn about these elders who seem to retain youthful characteristics way into old age? Those were the reasons I became interested in doing the book.

Wright

You discuss how great leaders in these two generations are often transformed in their very personal crucibles.

Bennis

What we really got out of this work was hearing people talk about those events in their lives that transformed them—their crucible experiences. In fact, I sometimes wish we had called the book *Leadership Crucibles*.

Wright

Can you give us an example that might help our readers understand what a crucible experience is?

Bennis

Being in a crucible is like when you're in a vortex of adversity, of challenge—often a loss of some kind. I'll give you several examples. Mike Wallace, founder of the television show *60 Minutes*, said that the crucible experience in his life was when his nineteen-year-old son, Peter, fell off a mountaintop in Greece and died. Wallace said at the time that it changed his life. He said, "Now I'm going to do what I really want to do," so he started *60 Minutes*.

Another example would be eighty-five-year-old Sidney Rittenberg, who is now running a consulting business in Seattle and helping U.S. companies develop businesses in China. Sidney, who ended up in China during World War II, became an advisor to Mao Tse Tung, Chou En-Lai and other Chinese leaders. Following the Cultural Revolution, these same leaders imprisoned him for thirteen or fourteen years. When he finally returned to the states in 1981, he became an entrepreneur. That experience of being in prison for all those years during the Cultural Revolution was what shaped him.

There's the case of Jeff Wilke, who's now a senior executive at Amazon.com. When he was working for AlliedSignal, a factory under his supervision burned down, and several people were killed. Wilke had to spend the better part of a week talking to their surviving family members. He realized as a result of that experience how important human life was, how business wasn't just about meeting the quarterly earnings report and that running a corporation was very much like being part of a community. It changed his whole outlook on leadership and management.

Then there's the story of Tara Church, who recently graduated from Harvard Law School. When she was eight years old, Tara and her Brownie troop were on a weekend hiking trip in the Los Angeles area. There was a drought in Los Angeles at the time, so the girls decided to take paper plates along, because they didn't want to use water to wash the plates and the other equipment they had. Then they realized that paper plates were made from wood, and they became worried about the deforestation going on throughout the world. Tara Church and about six or seven of her fellow Brownies started an organization in which groups of Brownies all over the country would start planting trees to make up for the trees lost to deforestation. They called themselves the Tree Musketeers, and it's now a national organization. Tara's mother is chairman of the board. They have an executive running it and plant about a million trees a year.

Wright

Dr. Bennis, many of our listeners work for companies that are struggling to cope with change. Individually, of course, it's a daunting task for professionals to change with the times, to adopt new ways of thinking or working. In my experience, it seems that it's almost unnatural for human beings to change significantly. What are your recommendations for helping people to move out of their comfort zones and to embrace change?

Bennis

That's a big and important question. I don't think change is necessarily something that's resisted at all times by all people. I think, in some cases, there are people who really anticipate, look forward to and thrive on change. And in this world, if they don't, they're going to miss the train. There's not an institution that I know, not a profession that I'm aware of, that isn't undergoing constant and spastic change. Change is now the constant. Even though it may not be a natural act for certain people, I think it's something that everyone has got to understand. Take education, for example. It's no longer just four years of college. Education is really turning into a process of lifelong learning. Universities are going to have to take responsibility not just for their alumni but for people in much older age groups, who have to keep learning because the half-life of professions is shrinking every day.

The way organizations must deal with change is by helping people realize that in the process of changing, they're going to benefit from all sorts of educational programs and opportunities. The people have to be *involved* in the change because if they are a part of the process, they're much less threatened by change. There are a lot of reasons why most people resist change, but among the most important is their reliance on old habits, especially the ones that have been successful. Related to that is self-esteem. If you're doing something extremely well, are pretty successful at it, getting a lot of rewards for it and your sense of self-esteem is based on your competence, it's got to be difficult if you're put into a totally different and new situation. Organizations have to help people get into a safe "holding pattern" where they can learn new skills without it being a threat to their self-esteem. So, to summarize, people have got to be *involved* in the change, they have got to be *informed* of the change, and they have got to be *educated* and put into a *safe holding area* where they're not going to be overly threatened by change.

Wright

I've noted that some leaders want to grow and improve. They've read about philosophies and strategies, but they strike out with ideas that are untested. How do you think an organization can ensure that it's getting the right kind of help before implementing new strategic initiatives?

Bennis

There are some vaunted organizations with good track records that can help out—the Conference Board, the American Management Association and a number of business schools and consulting firms, for example. They've already been "vetted," so to speak. If you're interested in finance, you would probably want help from places like Carnegie Mellon or the Wharton School or Stanford. If you're interested in overall management, you might want to bring in somebody from the Harvard Business School. There are also journals like the *Harvard Business Review*, the *MIT Sloan Management Review* and *Organization Dynamics* that people can read.

However, as a consultant, I have found that the problems presented to me are often too vague or not very clear. So the first thing a company should do, even before thinking about looking for a consultant, is identify which issues it needs help with. But I would like to add one more thing: There's usually enough wisdom and enough people in an organization who have the knowledge and the understanding to help solve a particular problem before seeking a consultant. One of the most important attributes of leadership is understanding and developing that talent. I really think that most people and most organizations have the inherent competence to solve their own problems without going outside.

Wright

In the late '70s and early '80s, I was writing a training course for a national franchise, and it was based on objectives. In almost everything that I read, the author was either commenting on something that you had written or just outright saying it himself. Did you have anything to do with management by objectives?

Bennis

The idea of management by objectives belongs to Peter Drucker. My own mentor, Doug McGregor, is another person who was very keen on the idea of not just management by objectives but the whole issue of "personnel evaluation." To work with the person you're trying to supervise, help, develop or coach was to work out the objectives together. Even today, if you were to say to Peter Drucker, "Leadership is important," he would ask, "Leadership for what?" There's always an objective for everything we should be doing.

Wright

With the complexity of today's business culture, how important is it for a leader to know how to measure the effectiveness of his strategies for growth and change?

Bennis

It's always useful to have metrics that really make a difference and to measure those as much as possible. The problem with metrics is that they are often too narrow, as with exclusively financial metrics. Often those things that are easier to measure mislead us because of the "fallacy of concreteness." For example, a company's earnings might seem concrete, but these days, even earnings are being questioned. The number of companies restating their earnings is extraordinarily high right now. So it depends on what metrics you're talking about, because some things are best understood through anecdotal or qualitative methods.

The important question to ask is, "What are the metrics that really make a difference?" For example, if we're going to look at organizations, we have to realize that they are also communities. So we wouldn't want to just measure financial results. In the long run, we might want to measure such things as the general climate of the organization or how much stress is present or how many opportunities for growth and development there are or how innovative the company is. We must also develop metrics for understanding how transparent an organization is. How much candor is there among employees? These are hard things to measure, but they can be more critical than short-term financial results. In fact, I believe that metrics like those have to augment quarterly reports on earnings. I'm not saying or advocating that earnings or financial data are not important; in the long run, of course, they have to be important.

Wright

A lot has been written about the rise and fall of technology companies in recent years. There are other glaring examples of poor leadership at the corporate level that have resulted in the bankruptcies of some of the nation's largest companies. It's as if many of these highly successful organizations never really understood what made them successful and, therefore, they couldn't replicate their success when the economy or the culture changed.

Bennis

I think that's absolutely true.

Wright

From your experience, what is the single most important consideration for companies seeking successful organizational change and improving results from their efforts?

Bennis

There are two major indicators by which organizations can be measured. They are my two big "A's." The first big "A" is alignment. How aligned is an organization? That is, at every level of the hierarchy, how are people aligned behind the mission and the vision and the strategy of the organization? Are the main driving mission and strategy understood at every single level? Are they acted on, and are they rewarded? The second "A" is adaptability, the extent to which an organization has the capacity to be agile, to be quick to take advantage of opportunities. The real trick of leadership, then, is getting an organization aligned behind changing strategies and missions. You see, if you just have alignment without adaptability, you've got an old-fashioned command-and-control, almost militaristic, organization. If you just have adaptability without alignment, you have a sort of anarchy in which no one knows what's going on. Both have to be yoked together, and leadership has to somehow create alignment with adaptability.

Wright

What a great half-hour this has been. Dr. Bennis, I really appreciate the time that you spent with me today.

Bennis

It was my pleasure, David. Thank you very much.

Wright

Today we've been talking with Dr. Warren G. Bennis, who is a distinguished professor of business administration at the Marshall School of Business and founding chairman of the Leadership Institute, both at the University of Southern California. He served for many years on the faculties of the Sloan School of Management at MIT, Harvard Business School and Boston University.

Warren Bennis
m.christian@marshall.usc.edu

Chapter 2

JACK LANNOM

Jack Lannom is a speaker, author, consultant, corporate coach, and master of Kung Fu. Jack has worked with many Fortune 500 companies. He is adept at conducting leadership, sales, customer service training, speaking on personal development, teaching learning and performance improvement skills, and delivering a motivational kick off. Jack's presentations are always a high energy, filled with laughter and rollicking good fun while they are filled with an enormous amount of content, instruction and practical application.

The Interview

David E. Wright (Wright)
Jack Lannom is an internationally known speaker, author and consultant who has served as a corporate coach for several Fortune 500 companies, including Citibank, R & R Donnelly and Sons, Jefferson Pilot Communications, Caterpillar and Knight Ridder newspapers. His most recent book, *Untapped Potential*, was published in 1998 by Thomas Nelson Publishers. Jack's PBS television program, *Lannom's Memory Methods*, ran for eleven years, the first and longest running series of its kind, inspiring millions of people in the United States and Mexico. He is the author of *Transformational Coaching,*

Quantum Mind: The Self Concept Game, Quantum Quality Management, Lannom's Memory Methods, People Power and *The Dynamics of Remembering Names and Faces.* Jack, welcome to *Mission Possible!*

Jack Lannom (Lannom)

Thank you, David. It's my honor to be here.

Wright

I was tempted to read two or three pages of your biography as part of your introduction, but I want our listeners to hear about your fascinating life from you. For example, in addition to being a professional speaker, author and consultant, you're quite an athlete, holding a black belt in six different styles of kung fu. Tell us a little about your background, Jack, including what you perceive to be the value of martial arts.

Lannom

I think the value of martial arts for a person, if you're under a good instructor, is not teaching you to be pugnacious and go out and misuse the art and try to hurt people with it. Rather, it's the discipline it affords. It's phenomenal discipline, David. It really teaches you how to focus, and that's so important in business. So I use it for business metaphors and business analogies. If we want to accomplish anything, it can't be scattered and it can't be with the shotgun approach; it has to be with the rifle approach. That's what kung fu has done for me. It's given me that ability, after doing it for thirty-eight years and becoming a master, to really focus on what I want to accomplish. When you've got a brick there before you and your grand master says, "Ah, you must break brick," then you ask, "Can I?" He says, "Yes you can. Just take and hit your hand through brick and hit my hand below the brick." Then you say, "But Grand Master, the brick is in front of your hand." He says, "Right. You go through brick and then hit my hand." Then I ask, "Well how do you do it?" He says, "You scream like crazy." Looking for some kind of kung fu secret, I say, "Why do I scream like crazy?" He says, "Because hurt like crazy." Chinese humor, you know. He taught me as a young person, starting when I was seventeen years old. It helped me with standing before literally thousands of people and putting on demonstrations with my kung fu teachers and during the halftime show of a hockey match in Nashville, Tennessee. As a young person standing before people, kung fu gave me a lot of confidence demonstrating the art and having the concentration and focus to do these techniques. It's been a wonderful discipline to apply in every area of my life.

Wright

Does your audience get involved in it?

Lannom

Oh yes. I have them do some of the moves and techniques, and it really helps them to learn how to focus also.

Wright

I also read that you hold the world's record for breaking a 3,150-pound block of ice with a single blow from your hand.

Lannom

That's right.

Wright

When you train U.S. marshals and FBI agents, I expect that feat gets their attention.

Lannom

Yes, it most definitely does. It enables them to learn some body and mind techniques. It teaches the body to relax and not be tense and how to flow. In the very tense situations they're in, many times, they lock up and their bodies lock up. We teach their minds to be relaxed in the very center of stressful situations. It helps them to stay in control. It's just like a doctor in the middle of an emergency situation in the ER center. In a very, very chaotic situation where people's lives are at stake, he has to be calm, and all the nurses are watching him control his emotions. I teach people how to be very calm and relaxed in a very tense situation with the martial arts. The stress techniques in this, David, are just invaluable for a person.

Wright

When we watch people on television who are breaking things for competition or the enjoyment of others, what you're saying is that they're actually releasing rather than getting tense to do that at the moment?

Lannom

That's right. They have learned techniques to relax themselves, and then all of a sudden, they explode and release all that stored energy. It's not an imploding inside of their being. It's an explosion, everything coming out just for that one second.

Wright

Jack, you've been described as having the energy and humor of Robin Williams. Do you find that people learn faster or better when humor is involved?

Lannom

Oh yes, David. When I was in college, I went through a period called inspirational dissatisfaction. I was listening to my teachers while they were instructing, and they were so boring. There was no passion in their teaching. Everyone was half asleep in my class. I was so dissatisfied by the way they taught that it inspired me to begin thinking that if I ever got to teach in college, which I did, I would never teach that way. It's called inspirational dissatisfaction. So I always teach with humor and passion. One of my teachers in high school said that if you're going to teach someone, if you're going to help him or her learn, fun learning is real learning; it's true learning. Make it enjoyable so that you will engage the mind. The limbic system is located in the center of the brain, and the limbic system is the emotional control center for the brain. So if you want to engage whole-brain learning when you're teaching others, you must get their emotions involved.

I have them laugh, get up and move around, and I have them give each other high fives. I use a lot of humor in my teaching so that the class will be memorable and enjoyable. I had one board member at a prestigious bank say, "Jack, I've heard about your humor and this tomfoolery you get into. Listen, these people are professionals. I wish you would please curb all that. We've got the president of the bank, the chairman of the board, all the key reports to the chairman. So please, in your two-hour seminar for these very professional people, please do not use your humorous style." I said, "I got you. I know exactly what you want." He left, and an hour later he came back in and they were all laughing their heads off. They were high-fiving, jumping around the room, and he said, "I would have never believed you could turn this group of stiff-necked bankers into a bunch of children running around and having fun at a board meeting."

Wright

Tell us a little bit about your *People First* presentation, especially the pyramid of people of power.

Lannom

The whole purpose of *People First* is to go against the grain of what's happening in America. We're taking companies and preparing them for Wall Street so everything should look good for the bottom line and then taking this out to the market makers for profit. So what we have today is profit first, not people first. What we're actually doing is sacrificing long-term relationships and partnerships on the altar of short-term gain and short-term profit. The whole concept of people first is saying that the greatest asset is our long-term, trust-based relationships. If we're going to really stay in the market and really be productive and profitable, it has to be long-term viability, and long-term viability is predicated solely on long-term relationships. It's relationships not only with your shareholders or your customers but your internal customers. So it's people first. The people you have in your company should become your purpose partners, not just employees. They are your partners, and it's all for a purpose. Put your purpose partners first, and then you will reap the profits, because profits are an inevitable outcome if you put people first.

The pyramid of people power teaches people an extraordinary system for extracting excellence from every person. It starts off with the five most important words you can say to the people in your organization and your external customers, which are, "I am proud of you." You want to be incessantly saying those five words as a leader: "I am proud of you." Going up the pyramid the four most important words you can say to a person are, "I believe in you." The three most important words you can say are, "I need you." The two most important words ascending the pyramid of people power are, "Thank you." The single most important word is "yes." YES stands for You Expect Success. This philosophy creates an air of expectancy that we're going to be successful because we've hired these successful people. We've got a successful product, successful service, successful principles and purpose, so we're all focused on YES. We're creating this transformational environment where it's, "Yes. Yes, we can do it. If it can be done, I can do it."

Wright

That could be effectively used in a parenting class.

Lannom

Oh yes, yes, yes. And it has. It's been used with parents for years and years.

Wright

Jack, you also talk about the BEST strategy as a leadership tool. I imagine that's some sort of an acronym. What is the BEST strategy?

Lannom

BEST is a way to bring the best out of people. "B" stands for "belief." It's really getting congruent with what our beliefs are. What are our core values? What are the things that we really believe? What's most important? You're focusing on those beliefs. If one of your beliefs is that people are your most important asset, then you want to show them that you believe in them.

"E" is a natural outgrowth of the belief, which is "environment." You want to create a transformational environment that truly elicits the untapped potential of everybody in the organization. You don't want to throw the kill switch on the human spirit; you want to turn on the human spirit. You turn it on by creating an environment that's safe, not an environment that's critical and condemning and cynical but one that celebrates the human spirit. It's so very important having a great environment.

Then the "S" stands for "systems," so you want to be thinking about how we're pointing a finger at people although maybe it's not a people problem; maybe it's a systems problem. Dr. Demming said that eighty-five percent of our problems are systems problems; only fifteen percent are people problems. What I believe is that we need to integrate the best business systems with the best human system. I think true success is looking at not only our human systems but also our business systems.

Then continuing with the BEST formula, the "T" in the system stands for "training." Training is investing in the greatest asset of our company, the minds of the people in the organization. Training and teaching means constant, continuous education. We need to have not only a CEO, a chief executive officer, but we need to have a CLO, a chief learning officer in the organization to make sure that we're growing intellectually. An organization needs to be constantly growing in the knowledge of its industry and in the knowledge of its competitors so that the company will remain competitive, productive and profitable. In a learning culture like this, where everyone becomes a learning monster, the organization crackles with passion and excitement. So a learning organization is really about building lives and passing on a legacy rather than building the loot and passing on lunacy.

Wright

You advocate learning how to promote long-term relationships. Could you give us some examples of how to do it?

Lannom

The best way to create long-term relationships is to learn about trust and that true long-term relationships are built on trust. If there's no trust, there is no relationship. You look at a marriage, and if a man's been unfaithful, rebuilding that marriage could take a long time, because the wife does not trust the husband any longer. In the same manner, if an employee has done something where some duplicitous activity has gone on, then it's hard for the employer to trust that employee. The employee has dealt a death blow to a trust-based relationship.

I believe that trust is predicated upon six different psychological elements, and they all begin with the letter C. The first element of trust is character. You have to have character because that's how you build long-term relationships where I can trust you. Moreover, there needs to be a sense of competency. If you have character but no competency, I can't trust you. You must possess character, then competency, and then you want to care. If there's caring, then you can trust in a person. In addition, if there is consistency in the behavior you can trust in them. And if there is good, clear, consistent communication, then this also fosters trustworthiness. Therefore, you need to have character, competency, caring, consistency and communication. The sixth "C" of trustworthiness is commitment. There has to be commitment. If there is commitment in a relationship, then it can build into a long-term relationship. It needs to be trust based. If it's trust-based and these are the six dimensions of trust, then we're going to have a long-term relationship and it's going to be a quality relationship.

Wright

That says a lot about some of the lifestyles that we have seen in the past few decades, where people are living together prior to marriage. Even if that hit on the first five "C's," it wouldn't stand the test of the sixth one, would it?

Lannom

That is right; it wouldn't at all. It's really interesting when someone says, "I don't really trust this person; I don't know what it is." You start asking if there's a character problem. "No, there's tons of character and integrity there." Then you ask if it's a competency problem, if the person lacks skills and knowledge. "No, he's very competent in knowledge, skills and experience. It's all there." Then you ask about caring. "That's it. He doesn't care. There's no caring for me. He never expresses how much he cares about me. That's it, Jack." When I ask those questions, I am consciously going through the six dimensions of trust to determine the particular trust issue.

Wright

I would say that change is probably the most difficult thing for any employee to do. Do you teach ways to implement change personally and within the organization?

Lannom

Yes, David, and that's a great question. I think this is probably one of the greatest issues facing us in this country, especially after 9/11/01. Everything's changed. This is the paradigm of this millennium. With all the change in technology, with all the changes we're facing in every area in this country, people are seeking ways to cope. How do I cope with change? I have a change formula that is very helpful, both in understanding change and initiating a change process.

The change formula states that "change is a function of need plus a philosophy plus a strategic plan that's greater than all the restraining forces." So when you're looking at your life, there has to be some kind of impetus for change—in other words, a need for change. If you don't identify the need for change, then there is no reason to change. If you draw a line at the bottom of a chalkboard and say, "That's where I am," and then you go up maybe fifteen inches on the chalkboard and say, "That's where I need to be," the greater the gap between where you are and where you need to be, the greater the dissatisfaction that you're experiencing in your life. If an individual or organization has not identified the need for change and everyone is not congruent and in alignment with the need for change consequently, there's not going to be any change. I don't care what needs to be changed, corporately or in a family or in an individual's life, the number one factor in initiating the change formula is need.

The next element in the change formula is philosophy. We have to put a philosophy in place. A philosophy is made up of three areas—values, mission and vision. I have to start with core values; that gives me my identity. The next aspect of a unified philosophy is a mission, a core purpose. The last aspect of a transformational philosophy is to have a vision that gives me a desirable future, an attractive destination. That's my philosophy. Hence, my philosophy becomes a driving force in my corporation and in my personal life.

The next element you must have in place is a strategic plan. You have to have a strategic plan in order to transform your change formula into a reality. The philosopher Seneca once said, "If a man does not know what harbor he's making for, no wind's the right wind." You've got to know what harbor you're making for. You have to have not only the peak but the path; which lays out the way to get to the peak. The path is the strategic plan to get there. Finally, all of these driving forces that you have in your change formula must be greater than all the restraining forces. We have to identify the restraining forces. Is it time? Is it money? Is it ego? Is it the marketplace? There you have it, David. That's my change formula.

Wright

That's very interesting. Some have said that the difference between leadership and management is vision. Would you agree with that?

Lannom

I think that there's a lot of truth in that; however, I think that's only part of the story. I think that today we're over-managed and under-led in every area of life. I think that the real area that separates leaders from managers is not just a vision but knowledge—knowledge of what's more important, what's less important and what's not important at all. Until you figure those three things out, you never know what's to be included in your plan, what's to be excluded in your plan, and you never know how you're doing.

Wright

You're not talking about product knowledge; you're talking about wisdom.

Lannom

Absolutely. I'm talking about wisdom. Solomon said, "Wisdom is a principle thing; therefore get wisdom." I believe that wisdom is knowledge of what is the most important thing. I believe what separates the leader from the manager is philosophy. The word "philosophy" is derived from two Greek words, *philos,* love and *sophos,* wisdom. So the literal definition of philosophy is "the love of wisdom." The true leader is philosophically empowered. His all-consuming passion is to impart that philosophy to everyone else. Therefore, true empowerment is philosophical empowerment. That's the foundation on which you can build a productive, profitable and passionate organization. It's the substructure on which you can build a great superstructure.

Wright

What are the ten core competencies that you teach in your presentation titled *The Leader's Leader?*

Lannom

The Leader's Leader is made up of ten integrated, mutually self-consistent core competencies. I use the word LEADERSHIP as an acrostic to help people remember the ten core competencies.

The first letter is "L", which stands for *logos.* It's a Greek word that stands for logic. *Logos* in the Greek language also means a complete system of thought. It can represent your total philosophy, your total world view. It gives meaning, purpose and significance to everything you do. It is the philosophical foundation for a leader; he's leading from something. In order to lead to something you must lead from something. This is the foundation. It becomes the theory, but theory without practice is dead. However, practice without theory is blind. The theory is the *logos,* and that's your logic, your reason to achieve, reason to believe. That's your very first core competency.

Next in our acrostic is the letter "E", which stands for example. You have to be an example of the *logos* or your philosophy. Whatever you lips are declaring, your life must be an example of it. There cannot be an integrity gap between your lips and your life.

The next letter in our system is "A", which represents the concept of authority. The principle of authority examines the leader's understanding of power and how he uses power. Here is a definition of power: Real power is the power that makes other people powerful. A leader doesn't have power to lord it over people or to hold power but to give it away, in order to empower people and make everyone around him powerful. The first three core competencies actually legitimize your leadership. You have a foundation that's truth in all things, wisdom in all things and excellence in all things. You have a great foundation, and you are an example of your foundation, that philosophy. Moreover, you have learned how to truly empower others. You're not out there intimidating people. Your leadership style is not about high command and high control. You're not throwing a kill switch every time you enter a room.

Let me ask you a question. Have you ever been in a situation where the room just lights up and glows and radiates when the leader walks out of it? Many leaders, unfortunately, are characterized by this attitude. In contrast, a good leader should want a room to light up and glow and radiate when he walks into it, not out of it.

The next letter in our system is "D". The letter "D" represents destiny, and destiny focuses the leader's attention on the visionary aspects of directing the company toward a desirable future state. There has to be a desirable destination, a worthy end state, in order to create future pull in an organization. Let us continue with our LEADERSHIP acrostic.

The letters "E", "R" and "S" stand for education, relationship, and systems. The actualization of these three core competencies brings to fruition your destiny or your vision. You must educate everyone in your philosophy, your *logos* in order to create unity. In addition, you need quality relationships that communicate to everyone, "We're all in this together, and there's a team here. We're all significant, we're all meaningful, and we all have a meaningful part in a meaningful mission." Therefore, trust-based relationships are the glue that keeps everything together. The letter "S" represents systems. Systems thinking teaches everyone to see everything in the organization as interconnected and interrelated. And understanding the interrelationship between education, relationships and systems enables a company to achieve and make its vision a reality.

The letters "HIP" in the LEADERSHIP acrostic are the outcome of the first seven core competencies. The letter "H" stands for happiness, which represents your culture. If a leader is leading properly with these core competencies, then the culture will be a happy one. In a happy culture, you don't see people that look like they're oppressed or get the feeling that the kill switch has been thrown on the human spirit. Everybody's fully human and fully alive in a happy environment.

The next letter in our acrostic is "I". The letter "I" represents ideation, and ideation means creativity. The leader needs to learn how to tap into everybody's creativity. The principle of ideation teaches the leader to challenge the known and defend the unknown. The primary attitude of ideation that is fostered by the leader states that there is nothing that's sacred. It says, "We can improve everything around here. We can make it better. We want all your ideas to make it better. You see things that I don't see. You're on the front line with the customers, and you know what customers want. How can we improve it? Be an owner. Own it and come back and tell me what we need to do. Be my eyes and ears. Let's all think together." Somebody said that eighty percent of the people don't think, fifteen percent think they think, and five percent think. The five percent who are the thinkers are asking the best questions. Some of the best questions focus on, "How can we improve this situation? How can be we make it better? We want to tap everybody's creativity." The greatest untapped resource in any organization is the creativity of the individual members.

Now we come to the last letter in our leadership system. The letter "P" represents, passing on a legacy. Let's teach people how to be great followers. Let's have a class on becoming a world class protégé, and let's build leaders. We have to be constantly building leaders. All the statistics that I've read in my life on many great companies state that they're usually built around a charismatic personality. When that person dies or leaves the company, the company dies because there was no succession plan. There's no leadership book in place, there's no model to pass on to successive generations. We're not teaching leadership principles to future leaders. We're not bringing up future leaders and teaching them how to lead. There's no modeling of or education of exemplary leadership, so when that leader goes, the company goes out of business. That's very, very sad. That's what is happening in every area of our lives.

Wright

One of your presentations, *You Are a Genius,* talks about new ways to learn faster and work smarter. Could you tell us a little bit about these ways?

Lannom

What we're missing in school, what we do not understand, is that we think that most of our educational problems are student problems and that we don't have any teaching problems. We're not really teaching the student to learn how they learn. People are different types of learners. We all don't learn the very same way. There's the visual learner, the auditory learner, the kinesthetic learner. The kinesthetic learner means you learn by being active. You move your body; you're a hands-on kind of person. If you have a person who can't sit still in the board room, he needs to move his body, get up and walk around or do something with his hands. The student may think you are sending the message, "We don't want you. Can't you be still?" The person wants to use his natural, inborn, God-given learning style, but your classroom isn't learning friendly. The whole environment is not learning friendly, and companies and schools are not learning friendly, because Johnny wants to move, and the teacher needs to realize that many of her students could be kinesthetic learners. We need to be wise enough to recognize the person's learning style.

Let's examine a familiar situation. A dad approaches his son, little Johnny, and attempts to teach him how to ride a bicycle. Dad's primary learning style is visual, his second style is auditory, and his last learning style is kinesthetic. He approaches Johnny and says, "Johnny, I want you to watch Daddy." Then he wants to tell Johnny about it, and then he wants to finally let Johnny get on and actually start to ride the bike. Well, the problem with this learning experience is that Johnny's learning pattern is kinesthetic, visual and auditory. First of all Johnny just wants to get on the bike. "Daddy, let me get on the bike." "Son, no, you've got to watch Daddy first." "I don't want to watch you. I just want to ride the bike." "Son, this is how you learn. Watch me first. Then I'll talk to you about it and then you can get on the bike." "Dad, I want to get on the bike first. Then I can watch you on the bike beside me, and then let's talk about it. I want to talk about it last. I want to get my hands on the bike first."

So there are all kinds of confusion going on in so many learning environments, because we're not even aware of the different learning styles. We're not honoring those different learning styles, and we're creating a lot of frustration. People are dropping out of formal education because they say, "It's not for me." It is for them if a teacher is wise enough to watch that student and say, "They have a different learning style from me and from everyone else in this classroom." Making it learning friendly is what I suggest—learning how to engage the whole mind. Make it fun. Make it something that has all these epiphanies. Find out people's interests. I have a lot of things I teach with—not just learning styles but learning techniques that we can learn much faster.

Wright

Jack, this has been a great learning experience for me, and I certainly appreciate you being with us this morning. If you had any parting words to say to someone who was trying to be better, to educate themselves more intelligently, what would you say to them?

Lannom

I would say to them that one of the most important things that they could do in their life is to get wisdom. Solomon said, "Wisdom is supreme; therefore get wisdom." In your life, you're going to need somebody to give you advice. You want to find people that have wisdom and give you wise advice. You may think, "That person has his Ph.D. Surely he'll give me wisdom." Or "That person is a multimillionaire. Undoubtedly he'll give me wisdom." But just because you're a millionaire or have your Ph.D. doesn't necessarily mean that you are wise; they don't necessarily go hand in hand. I've met some people that do not even have a high school education, and they were very poor, but they were the wisest people I've ever met in my life. Contrary to popular opinion, they were the richest people, because they were rich in wisdom and spirit, where it really counts.

Wright

Thank you very much, Jack, for being with us today. Jack Lannom is an internationally known speaker, author and consultant. His most recent book, *Untapped Potential,* was published in 1998 by Thomas Nelson Publishers, and you might want to consider going out and getting a copy. Thank you so much for being with us today, Jack.

Lannom

Thank you, David. It was truly my pleasure.

Jack Lannom
14050 NW 20 Street
Pembroke Pines, Florida 33028
Fax: 954.392.1533
E-mail: Jacklannom@aol.com

Chapter 3

TERRY PAULSON, PH.D.

Dr. Terry Paulson is a past president of the National Speakers Association and has attained its certified speaker designation. Along with Ronald Reagan, Colin Powell and Norman Vincent Peale, he has been inducted as a lifetime member of the CPAE Speakers Hall of Fame, an honor given to only 156 speakers worldwide since its inception in 1977. Terry's humor, down-to-earth style and practical insights have made him one of the country's most highly rated presenters.

The Interview

David E. Wright (Wright)
Today, we're talking with Dr. Terry Paulson, who is a licensed psychologist and author of the popular books Paulson on Change, They Shoot Managers Don't They?, Making Humor Work, 50 Tips for Speaking Like a Pro and Can I Have the Keys to the Car? He hosted ECI's business television series entitled Quality from the Human Side and is honored to be a distinguished faculty member of the Institute for Management Studies. His presentations help organizations, leaders and teams make change work. In over twenty-five years as a professional speaker and trainer, Dr. Paulson has presented to organizations such as IBM, Warner Brothers, Sears, 3M, Shering, Merck, AT&T, Federal Reserve Bank, Texaco, KPMG, US Steel,

NASA, PricewaterhouseCoopers and hundreds of universities, hospitals and associations. Terry Paulson, welcome to *Mission Possible!*

Dr. Terry Paulson (Paulson)

It's great to be with you.

Wright

As book titles go, *They Shoot Managers, Don't They?* ranks as one of the most interesting titles I've read. Could you tell us a little about what the book is about?

Paulson

The book captures one of the compelling insights into change. Change brings with it a certain amount of conflict. You're going to have some people who love change and some people who resist it entirely. That tension is something that people have to manage. We both honor the past, because it's something that we can learn a tremendous amount from. But it can't be an automatic veto to the kinds of changes that corporations and associations need to make. The book is about how to manage yourself and how to lead people in the midst of change. I think that's a struggle that almost everybody goes through. I try to bring a perspective that balances an appreciation for the past, at the same time constantly being open to how we can improve and having a little bit of fun in the process. The title reflects that, I think.

Wright

I've noticed that other speakers and authors whom I've heard and read in the past ten to fifteen years talk a lot more about balance than they used to. Why do you think that is?

Paulson

I think one of the most interesting things about life is that balance or tension—finding a way to take one's job seriously and at the same time take one's life seriously. It's the same thing with change. Change has an appreciation for the past, but it has to be open to anything in the future that I can do better. One also is challenged with the realities in our current economy, with the challenge of containing costs and at the same time investing where it counts. The balance issue, I think, really is a tension concept. If you ever let one side of your life become too predominant, you're not going to get the full benefit of what that balance can do for you. I think balance is an earned concept that everybody is trying to focus on in their own unique way, and I try and do the same thing when I talk to organizations or write books to deal with change.

Wright

Terry, allow me to quote you, if you don't mind. You say, "Learn to manage yourself before you lead others." What kind of self-management are you talking about, and where do people get this kind of information?

Paulson

I think one of the challenges that leaders face is that they are challenged to lead people in the midst of change. But many times, they're not totally sold on the change process themselves. They oftentimes are also looking for approval from the very people whom they need to lead. I'm sure you can relate to the fact, as a parent, that very few times when you're doing the right thing are you going to be 100 percent supported. I've never heard my son say to me, "Thank you, Dad, for disciplining me. I really needed that." In fact, if he did, I'd probably send him to therapy. What happens in the midst of change is that sometimes you have to be a catalyst for that change, and I would rather be respected than liked. Unfortunately, many people are oftentimes looking for approval, and that's where the self-management issues become critical for people. I have to learn to manage my own self-confidence, effectively balance that ability to catch myself with the ability to give appropriate self-criticism. Self-criticism is essential in a changing environment. Leaders no longer have all the answers, and if they have ego needs or ego problems, they resist change. They don't want to hear ideas unless they are their own ideas. What we try to challenge people to do is talk to themselves differently about leadership in a way that will allow them to be more open to the best ideas, no matter where they surface.

Those are challenges that a lot of leaders need help with, and there are a number of different sources. What I try to do is provide a realistic challenge for leadership to look at what they can do to manage their own motivation.

Wright

I heard a great educator in Texas many, many years ago say that management is self-management applied to others, which made a lot of sense to me. But it sure is hard to manage yourself.

Paulson

I think one of the real challenges of life is that when we are growing up, we are receiving messages about what we're not supposed to do—a lot of no's, a lot of correction, a lot of feedback. We begin to internalize that. In fact, some of the studies that have been done in this area have found that the average person is eighty percent internally critical and less than twenty percent supportive. If you're eighty percent critical to twenty percent supportive, you need a lot of support just to break even.

My theory is that the only time you will ever get that amount of support is when you're dating. That's the sales phase of a relationship. You hear, "I love you. You're wonderful. I really appreciate being with you." But as soon as you move into real life, most of the focus is on things that are wrong and things that you've made mistakes with. Likewise, we talk to ourselves in a way we would not talk to other human beings. The real challenge is how do you turn some of that around? I try to get people to, on a daily basis, instead of just focusing on the negatives at the end of the day, ask what they have done that day that's made a difference. It helps in our transition from work to know that we can take a little bit of time to focus on that positive dimension. As your educator had mentioned, that's the same kind of thing we ought to be doing with our people.

Most people are defined by the questions they are consistently asking as leaders. Most leaders only focus on the problems. They're running around to their people asking, "Got any problems? Got any problems? Any problems over here? Back to work!" The best leaders

I've ever known knew the importance of taking time to ask questions that focused on what was working. What's working for you? The first time you ask that question, they know you've been to a seminar or listening to a tape. But if you keep asking that question, all of a sudden, people begin to be aware of what's working and what they're doing to make a difference. Tom Peters used to ask, "What are you doing differently?" The first time you ask that, they know you've been to a seminar. If you keep asking that question, they know you them to be aware of what they're doing differently and begin to build on some of that positive dimension. I think that starts when leaders are able to do that with themselves and then model it in how they talk to other people.

Wright

You talk a lot about change. Everyone says change is inevitable. Why do you think it's so hard to change?

Paulson

It's one of those great tensions again. Life almost requires us to establish mastery, and we work very hard to develop new skills that allow us to be effective. Once we've reached mastery, we are bored unless we have new changes that come in, and yet we have a tremendous pressure to do things perfectly. It's one of those things I call the "imposter phenomenon." In fact, there's been research on this area as well. Seventy to eighty percent of Americans have imposter feelings. They're not imposters. People would rate their performances as effective, but inside they say to themselves, "If anybody found out how much I don't know about what I'm doing, I'd be in deep trouble, so at least I'd better dress for success."

The challenge to me is how to continue to establish mastery over the things that count but then get out of my comfort zone to know that I'm not alone. Everybody has these feelings of inadequacy, and change brings those to light. As soon as you have to go through change, you're aware of what you don't know. A lot of the resistance to change is my really wanting to stay in my comfort zone so that you'll know that I'm really good. As soon as I have to go through change, I have to go through error, and I've got to go through the challenge of doing it differently. Yet that's where the real excitement is. One of the most exciting times in our careers is when we're doing things that we're not entirely comfortable with. We look back on those and say, "Those are the good old days. I had to learn and master that." We want both mastery and change, and the tension is one of those things we have to deal with all our lives.

People are always coming to me and saying, "You've done your change program. Have you changed it?" That downright upsets me, because I've got to change my own program as I go through. We will always have that tension of mastery and overcoming boredom and learning new things. It's one of the things that create the dynamic of the journey of change.

A lot of people want to treat change like it's a movie. Let's take two and a half hours, learn this, and I'll be done. As soon as you get into one change, they're announcing new changes. People have to realize that the change process is more like a soap opera than it is a movie. The better off we are at constantly continuing to reinvent ourselves, the more likely it is that we will be valuable to our companies and that we'll be able to lead people through change. When somebody comes to leaders and says, "When are we going to be through with all this change?" I want leaders to say, "We're not! Get excited. You'll never be bored again. We're all in this together." We've got to have the areas where we have mastery, and we have to learn new skills that will allow us to be masters of skills that are needed in the future. It's a never-ending process, but it's also tremendously exciting.

Wright

I've got a daughter who's forty-one, a son who's forty and daughter who's a fourteen year old. I've thought that I had this parenting thing down, but I was wrong. So many things have changed during that twenty-five-year period in between that I really had to reconsider everything that I'd ever even dreamed about being a parent.

Paulson

It's not just the ages that we go through but the differences between kids. All you have to have is multiple children and you begin to realize that there is no one set way of dealing with situations. We constantly have to be open to new ways of handling things and at the same time learn from past traditions. There are those things we can do as parents that are effective, and it's the same way with leadership. Some of the things that used to work at the turn of the century are probably still working today, but we've got to be open to new things that will allow us to do them that much better. It's always that challenge of being ready to be re-taught. It's going to be with us, and that's what makes life exciting. I love it.

Wright

Many years ago, I was in one of your audiences in a session on humor. I laughed throughout the entire session and was smart enough to take notes that you call "takeaways." With all that's happened to the American business community over the past few years, why don't more companies use humor in the workplace?

Paulson

Whether or not they say they do, they do. It's one of the stables of sales. People use humor to bring joy into a conversation, and then they get the hearing that allows them to make their point and make sales. It's one of the reasons salespeople use it. One of the most attractive characteristics of people we enjoy living with and working with is a sense of humor. It brings perspective. I think one of the things all of us go through is bad days. Take somebody who, all of a sudden, in the midst of such a day, can say, "Some days you're the bug; some days you're the windshield." All of a sudden, we laugh, we get our perspective, we realize we're going to go through this. At the same time, it inspires us to get back into the process. There have been all kinds of research to indicate that it's effective in helping people increase their creativity. It's one of the stress tools that we use in handling the demands of the job. All of those are reasons that humor will always find its place.

I'm also quick to add that I take my job very, very seriously. I take my relationships seriously. But I take myself lightly. It's a big difference between using humor appropriately and using it inappropriately. I think that when you're making fun of others, the fun goes out of it. I'm always saying that the safest target for humor in a business environment is always yourself. Your ability to laugh at yourself creates an awareness that we all go through a certain amount of error. We all go through difficult times. Pope John XXIII said, "I sometime awake at night to think about a serious problem and decide I must tell the Pope about it. Then I wake up completely and remember that I am the Pope." I love that. I think every leader, every parent at times wakes up and thinks, "I'm going to ask somebody," and then they realize, "I am the person. I'm supposed to be asked." That's one of the values of humor. It allows us to keep our perspective.

Wright

When you work with corporations and organizations on the topic of humor, do you find that the ones where management opens everything up for a more humorous view of things excel any greater than those that don't?

Paulson

I think there are studies, and work has been done on the advantages of humor, and I wouldn't go through all of those stories. I certainly know of individuals who don't have much of a sense of humor who have still been very effective. I just think it's an added skill set. When you use it, it's a great bridge builder. It creates comfort. In a world going through increasing stress and demands, it's one of those things that, when we add it to our repertoire, just makes work a little bit more enjoyable. At the same time, it allows us to bounce back more quickly from some of the difficult times that we're going through.

Wright

I remember seven or eight years ago finding a book that you had written, published by the Crisp Publications—Making Humor Work. I used that book as reading material for my entire company. We went through it like a seminar. It really did lighten things up. During that period of time, people got closer together and go to know each other a little bit better.

Paulson

And knew each other in a fun way. People talk about training all the time, but you've just highlighted one of the best ways to go through training. Read a book together, talk about it in a staff meeting, and realize that the insights that you learn in the midst of that are the keepers that will allow you to have a focus for a given amount of time. The frightening thing is that sometimes, we fail to go back to it. I think there are a lot of great books that we've read at one time and need to review again, because we pull together some of those keepers, and they allow us to have a distinct advantage.

Wright

I just remembered. It's not "takeaways" that I learned from you seminar; it's "keepers"!

Paulson

No matter what you call them, I believe very strongly that every time you listen to something, every time you read something, you want to pull out your takeaways or your keepers and review them. When people take the time to review them, they work on a really powerful basis.

Wright

Your book *Can I Have the Keys to the Car? How Teens and Parents Can Talk About the Things that Really Matter* is an honest look at real problems. What led you to write it?

Paulson

Actually, I've got to give credit to my son. He came to me at the age of sixteen and said, "Are you going to buy me a car?" I said, "No, I'm not going to buy you a car." He said, "Everybody gets a car." I said, "It will be everybody minus one." He had not saved his money. He spent it on things. He'd save for a while and then spend it. I said, "You invested it in the wrong CDs. You've got to find a way to not only make money but to save some for the things that are important to you." I challenged him to come up with an idea that he could do. He was going to work and do some other things, and then he said, "I'm going to write a book." I said, "What's your book going to be?" He said, "It's going to be Favorite Family Lectures." I said, "That will probably sell." He said, "Yeah, you've given me a lot of lectures. Some of them are funny. I don't think parents know what to say, so I'm going to interview the kids and find out what the best lectures are."

We worked together over the course of a three-year period to interview teens and parents to find out what the most important life lessons are. He published his first book, *Secrets of Life Every Teen Needs to Know*, which is no longer in print. He made enough sales on that to get a car, and then he challenged me later to go back and rewrite it. We put together that particular book to give parents and teens a tool for talking about the things that matter.

It's amazing to me how we don't take quality time to talk about life lessons as kids are growing up. It used to be that we would have conversations. Now everybody has their independent life. They're all watching television, and they're getting inundated with things that don't really relate to the values that are important to life. My son and I ended up having wonderful conversations, just because we were going through the exercise. One mother told me that she used the book when she and her family taking vacations. Instead of listening to the radio or music, they would read a chapter, and when they stopped, they would discuss it—the husband, wife and kids. They would talk about how they felt about things, what the different approach was. Not that every one of the things that's in the books is the way to do things, but it certainly gets a conversation rolling about the things that are really critical in life—everything from sex to responsibility to doing well in school to faith to a variety of different areas. It gives parents and teens a chance to talk about things when they matter. If kids don't have that grounding, they haven't any moral compass. They haven't anything to counter with when they go out there into the world. They have challenges and difficult decisions coming up right and left.

Wright

Did you learn anything about your son Sean through that exercise that you didn't know before?

Paulson

He would say to me, "I wouldn't normally say anything, but my name's going to be on this book, too, so we can't put such-and-such in there." We ended up having conversations we probably wouldn't have had, because we were going through the journey together. I realize, as a parent, that we just don't have those quality conversations sometimes. Whether one uses the book or one starts to take the opportunity to discover the wisdom that has come through the ages, we need to take time to discuss it. There will be changes, just as you mentioned. Different generations have different challenges they've got to face. There are also some things that, if they learn them, are going to make their lives a lot easier, because they will have the respect, the character and the integrity to weather the journey through some challenging times.

Wright

After September 11, 2001, you wrote an article titled "Freedom Isn't an American Birthright; It's Earned." I understood it to be a commentary on the important things we must do as Americans. Were you asked to write it, or did you write it out of real concern?

Paulson

I think everyone will always remember where they were on September 11, 2001. I was actually in upstate New York, at Niagara Falls, on the U.S. side, doing a program for Verizon. I had not yet had a chance to even start to speak when we got word that the tower had been hit. Verizon's corporate headquarters was about three blocks away, so it was decided very quickly that we would cancel the meeting. People had to leave to help in getting the phone systems back up in that area. As we came out, we watched on TV as the plane crashed into the second tower and realized the severity of what was going on. Everybody else had a job to go to. I live in Los Angeles, and I was in

Mission Possible!

Niagara Falls. You don't realize how big this country is until you can't fly. I, along with many Americans, was apart from my family.

I had the opportunity to be in a hotel right across from Buffalo, waiting for the next plane to take off. With me was a group of teenagers that was now unable to go on a tour, and there was a group of World War II Navy veterans who were there for a reunion that weekend and weren't able to get out. Here you had teenagers, World War II Navy veterans and me. We were watching the events unfold, and I saw conversations between generations I know we would never have had prior to that time.

I wasn't asked to write something, but I felt compelled. I have two e-zines that I send out, and I write a lot of op-ed pieces for various newspapers. I decided that I wanted to write about what individuals can do. One of the things that I feel strongly is that the depression of our age is a learned helplessness, an attitude that says, "Nothing I can do makes any different in what happens, so I might as well wait until they do it to me; then we can sue them." What happens is that people have training in powerlessness, and that event on September 11 was such an attack that people were sitting back, feeling powerless. I felt that I needed to write something that would allow them to focus on what was in their control. I thought about what we could do as individuals to make a difference, all the way from raising flags to investing in U.S. stocks to taking time to be with our faith families and with our families and friends, giving blood. I saw people standing in line in Buffalo, ready to give blood. I have a flagpole in our yard, and we fly a flag on a regular basis, but I was away from home, so I went out and bought a flag. The people of Buffalo were honking their horns and waving, and I was raising the flag. I actually ran faster, because I felt compelled, now that I was representing the United States, to run faster. I almost killed myself getting back to the hotel with the flag, but I felt so proud. If Osama Bin Laden and those who were involved in this attack had known what it would do to create resolve and create a sense of togetherness and a reaffirmation of the things that we value most, they would never have carried it out. The cost of it was dear, and I don't discount those lost. At the same time, I think that what has come out of it is an appreciation for who we are as a country and for the values we do hold dear. I thin it was a wake-up call that I wanted to talk about, so I indeed wrote that particular piece. I have a Web site, unitedwecanwin.com, and that particular op-ed piece is there. If your readers and listeners look at op-ed pieces, they will probably get the opportunity to read it.

Wright

I have a copy of it. I think I went to terrypaulson.com to get it.

Paulson

Yes, if they go back into the archives of my e-zine, they can also find that title. The point I want to make to your people is that the value we have in this country, the commitment to capitalism and the commitment to the principles that make us who we are were attacked on that particular day. It's interesting that business was attacked. The real challenge is that since that time, we have had an opportunity to show that we are far bigger than any building that you can take down. It's the opportunity for small business and large business to work together to keep a system afloat and to continue to give people the American dream. I speak all over the world, and one of the things that is always interesting to me is how many people have said to me, "You know, the American dream isn't just for Americans. It's for all of us." It's a place where we've made it happen. We've been under attack, we're responding, and we have to continue to respond, because it isn't over as far as I'm concerned.

Wright

Like everyone else, I have read so much of what has been written. Your piece goes a little bit further. You talk about flying Old Glory and giving blood, but on the other hand, there are some other things that caught my attention. For example, there are ten things that you say we can do. One is to start a solo on your own or join in singing "America the Beautiful." Don't worry if you can't sing. God gave you the voice, and you deserve to hear it. Write President Bush and Congress to support them. You know, that would be cleansing in itself—writing the president to support him.

Paulson

The interesting thing is that more people are taking action. Over the long haul, one of the things that they've started to study more is "What is optimism?" Martin Seligman, who was the president of the American Psychological Association, challenged all the psychologists when he was president. He said that we know more about pathology than we know about health and that it's about time we put a little bit more time into positive psychology and start to look at those things that, when people do them, they become more empowered, they become more alive. He found out a lot about optimism, how optimism isn't Pollyanna thinking. It's a track record of overcoming obstacles. We, in many ways in our society, have been buying a bill of goods that says we need to make it easier on kids. It's exactly the opposite. The more kids are challenged, the more schools challenge people and the more likely it is that they gain the ability to have resilience and resolve. Our parents went through the Depression. It didn't make them weaker. It made them stronger, because they know what they're capable of doing. I think 9-11 did the same thing.

What I tried to do in that article was help people realize that we're not victims. There were victims; those are the ones who are dead as a result of that attack. But we are survivors, and survivors, by their actions, no matter what it is that they do, bring back control to their lives, and all of a sudden they gain renewed confidence and strength to bounce back. I challenged people in that article right away to get busy doing something, whether it was writing and singing, whether it was giving blood. I don't care what that is; when you get involved in action, you get an opportunity to gain back your strength, confidence and resolve. It was one of Yogi Berra's great lines: "When you come to the fork in the road, take it." It's not sitting back, doing nothing and moaning and complaining. Get involved in what you can, where you are, to make a difference, and the power comes back. We've seen that so much in terms of the giving that people did after 9-11, and the response that people had to that was empowering.

This is an amazing country, with people who have made it strong. I think no one will travel the same way in American again. In fact, Southwest Airlines was the first one to fly out of Buffalo, and I was on it. They were heading to Vegas, and I said, "I'd rather get to Vegas than stay in Buffalo." We were checking each person out. I don't care what you call it—profiling or whatever. We were all looking around and saying that if anyone starts to take over this plane, we're going to do our part. I think that's the attitude. Americans realize it isn't just our military that does things; everybody plays a role, like when Todd Beamer said, "Let's roll." I think that's the exciting part of what has come out of this that will be with us far longer than even the costs of the terrible attack.

Wright

With our *Mission Possible!* talk show and book we're trying to encourage people in our audience to live better and to be more fulfilled by listening to the examples of our guests. Is there anything or anyone in your life that has made a difference for you and helped you to become a better person?

Paulson

Wow, there are so many people who have come at the right time in my life who've had an impact. I would have to say that my father is one of those people. He was a man who achieved a lot in the business area, going all the way from working with Allstate Insurance and handling some of their computer processing challenges to becoming a financial officer for another firm when he retired from Allstate. He was a strong man of faith and had a tremendous sense of humor. It's the "fruit doesn't fall too far from the tree" aspect of life. He was a man who not only took his work environment very seriously but also his faith and his sense of humor and his family commitment. We still go back to our family reunions in Illinois. He'd send me back to the farm to work to have experiences. I think it brings to mind how the modeling that we do as parents is critical. I can think of how my dad handled things and know that if I use him as an example, it would be a powerful one.

I also had teachers who helped me. I had one teacher who challenged me my senior year. The first paper I got back from this woman had red marks all over it as well as a C minus. I was playing football, so I had written this paper the night before. I wasn't used to getting a C minus. I went up to her and said, "I'm a little concerned." She looked at me and said, "I don't think you're used to this, are you Terry?" I said, "No, I'm not. I usually get pretty good grades." She said, "Well, I know you're capable of it, and this paper shows that you are, but this paper looks like you did it last night." I remember looking at her like, "Oh, no. She knows!" She said to me, and I'll never forget it, "Terry, I want you to know something. I think you're capable of being a good writer, and I'm going to challenge you more than I challenge some of the other kids. I'm going to be tougher on you." In today's world, I'd probably call my lawyer and sue her! But in that environment, she challenged me to take it to another level. She also challenged me to compete for the competition to speak at graduation. I told her I didn't think I could do that. She said, "Terry, you've got a gift. You go out and do that." I will remember Mrs. Nayson for a long time, because she cared enough to challenge me.

I should also mention the first manager I ever reported to at Stanford Linear Accelerator. Jack Nichols was his name. I helped build a model of an electron microscope there. Every single week, he took a fifteen-minute walk with each one of his direct reports. I was the only summer employee he had, and he took a walk with me on a Friday. He said, "Terry, every week I walk with my people." I didn't know what bosses did, so now I was finding it out. They walk with people. I walked with this guy, and he said, "Terry, you've been here a week now. What's working for you?" That is a question I have used in leadership and in speaking ever since that day, because he caught me off guard. As a teenager, nobody ever asked me what worked. I was glad we were walking, and I finally came up with something. I said, "The guys taught me how to load the trucks." He said, "I'm glad you learned from the guys, but I want you to know that this summer, I expect to learn something from you. I'm going to ask you this question every week."

I felt like he was crazy. I felt like he ought to talk to my mom. She'll know I don't know anything, and she'll give me an excuse note. He asked me that question every week, and as a result of that, I learned something about leadership. It's the questions that you consistently ask that really convey what's important to you. Every week I had to have an answer. It's like with teachers. You learn how they give a test, and then you do well by studying that way for the test. He taught me every single week that I had to have a good idea. Twice that summer, he liked my idea so much that he said, "Terry, why don't you share that with the rest of the group?" I was intimidated, because I was seventeen, and the rest of them were old—thirty and thirty-one! At the end of the summer, he said, "You taught me something, Terry, and if you ever need a job, you come back here." I hold that man in the back of my brain as a mentor and as a model, because he believed that I could do something significant.

I think one of the key impressions we sometimes give people is, "Oh, what do I know?" I have a tremendous confidence that the people who are listening to this tape and the people who are involved in any leadership role have people who are working for them who know things that are just exceptional. But we don't ask the questions and take time to listen to get some of those great ideas. Those are people who made a difference in my life. I've tried to emulate the challenges, the humor and the aspiration to do something that is significant. Secondly, I have never forgotten that every person I meet is going to give me something that I can learn from if I take the time to listen.

Wright

Whatever these people did, it certainly worked. You're one of the finest educating conversationalists I've ever talked to. Can you imagine we're at the end of our time?

Paulson

That's what happens when you get talking!

Mission Possible!

Wright

Today, we have been talking with Dr. Terry Paulson, who is a psychologist, the author of several books and, as you have found out today, a great teacher and human being. Terry Paulson, thank you so much for being with us today on *Mission Possible!*

Paulson

Thank you very much for letting me join in, and it certainly is a mission possible. Let's keep that possibility going every single day.

Dr. Terry Paulson
Paulson and Assoc., Inc.
28717 Colina Vista
Agoura Hills, California 91301
Phone: 818.991.5110
Fax: 818.991.9648
E-mail: terry@terrypaulson.com

Chapter 4

SAM ALLMAN

Sam has been one of the most in-demand sales speakers and trainers. Delivering high content, customized, inspiring programs in areas such as leadership, customer service, management development, team building, and retail sales. He has helped organizations bring their employees and managers to a higher level of productivity and performance. He captivates his audience by using humor, enthusiasm, extensive knowledge and expertise. Sam Allman contributes monthly articles to websites and magazines.

The Interview

David E. Wright (Wright)

Today we're talking with Sam Allman. Sam began working at the age of nine, installing carpets with his father. He continued working in the floor covering business as a salesman in his twenties, as a store owner in his thirties and as territory manager, district sales manager and vice president at Mohawk Industries in his forties. Working from his principles, Sam has teamed with major corporations to create corporate universities that have transformed training from a cost center to a profit center. He currently is dean of Mohawk University. He's taught managers how to lead, manage, supervise, motivate and coach. He's taught sales employees how to increase sales, sales mar-

Mission Possible!

gins and customer loyalty. Sam received his four-year BS degree from Long Beach State University and his master's degree from Brigham Young University. Today, he leads Allman Consulting and Training Company. His clients include Mohawk Industries, Home Depot, Lowe's and Sears. Sam, welcome to *Mission Possible!*

Sam Allman (Allman)

Thank you. It is great to be here.

Wright

You have written that success eludes people for two basic reasons: They can't find the correct principles or they can't apply correct principles to resolve their challenges. Can you explain to our listeners and to our readers what you mean?

Allman

Yes. Many speakers and authors of self-help books try to simplify the path to success. In their simplifying, they may teach correct principles, but they fail to recognize or acknowledge that success may be achieved by different paths—and sometimes opposing paths. These speakers and authors provide a favorite success formula—one they've simplified for easy application. The catch is that success is not that simple. These authors don't realize that we can succeed by applying one principle in one situation and yet succeed equally well by applying an opposite principle in a different situation. When leaders must apply one principle in one case and its opposite principle in another case, the leader faces a paradox. Instead, these authors tell us to "go out and do this." Certainly, their formula works with some of the people some of the time but not with all of the people all of the time. Success hinges on the wise application of correct principles. I find that to succeed as a manager, you have to be able to apply two correct opposing principles—sometimes at the same time. That's why our leadership literature is bursting with contradictory advice. One author says solve it one way while another tells stories of successful leaders who did exactly the opposite. So managers who are trying to learn to lead better often get confused. They may use too much of one principle and not enough of the other. Leadership is actually very difficult and very complex. It's much more difficult than it appears. It may appear easy, but it's difficult to apply successfully, because you're trying to blend two quite different and opposing principles.

Wright

Also, you talk about inescapable paradoxes. What are some of these paradoxes, and do these paradoxes always impede the decision process?

Allman

Let me explain. In all fields of endeavor, whether in leadership, parenting or relationship building, almost every success principle has a contradictory counterpart. That's a paradox: something that's true and effective yet contradicts something else that's also true and effective. It's confusing. I'll give you an example. One set of opposing true principles is self-confidence at one end and humility at the other. A leader should be self-confident. Indeed, how would you feel if your doctor said, "You need your appendix out, and I think I can do it." You don't want somebody like that. You want someone who believes he can do it.

Wright

Right.

Allman

The paradox is that while you must be confident of your abilities, at the same time, you have to be humble and always willing to learn more. If you're not teachable, you're not learning and you're not open to influence. Cornell University studies found that people who think they know it all—to the point of being overly self-confident—are actually incompetent. Their self-confidence has inhibited their learning. The arrogant usually have an answer for everything, but it's really a sign that they have stopped learning.

Wright

So how do successful managers blend this paradox?

Allman

It's not easy, because almost every success principle has its opposite. Niels Bohr once said, "The opposite of a true statement is a false statement. However, the opposite of a true principle may very well be another true principle." That's what makes leading and parenting so difficult. Let me give you an example from parenting: I'm a father of ten children.

Wright

Wow!

Allman

Yes, they've taught me a lot. I've learned that fathering is a great challenge yet wonderful at the same time. I've found that a principle that worked with one child often didn't work with another. With some of my children, I needed to be very authoritative. Let me explain what I mean by that. "Authoritarian" implies dictatorship, while "authoritarian" in this case implies clear rules enforced consistently, with an abundance of love for the child. Some children needed more structure, more control. With other children of mine, I needed to empower them more. Was there one right answer for all? No, because each child was different. Besides that, at different ages, they needed different parenting approaches. One answer never worked for all children, at all ages, in all situations. One of the metaphors I find helpful is taking a shower. In order to take a comfortable shower, we need the right combination of cold and hot water. We get that by adjusting the knob until we get the temperature just right. I call that "finessing" the hot and cold until we have the right combination. Then, the shower feels comfortably warm. Of course, a temperature that feels comfortable to me might feel too cold or hot for my wife. That's part of the finessing process. Now, we are enjoying our shower, and then somebody flushes a toilet or starts the washer. You've had that happen?

Wright

Absolutely.

Allman

The shower situation has changed, so we have to adjust, or finesse, the knob again to get the right combination for the new situation—adjust it so it works for us. Let me apply this finessing idea to a few examples of common paradoxes. Think about the challenges you've had and see if my recommendations might work for you. One set of opposing principles that we teach in leadership is the importance of having a vision of a better tomorrow versus the unavoidable fact that we can only work in today. Vision is vital. Great leaders are forward thinkers. They think about the future and have a vision of what they want the group to achieve. The paradox is that you can work only in today. So how can you create your ideal future when you only have today? My recommendation: Live today as if it were your last, yet live in faith as though there will be a great future and as if you are responsible for creating that great next step in your life. You have to live in the moment, but how do you live in the moment and still be a visionary? Many of us postpone our happiness. We say, "I'll be happy when I acquire this or do that. I'll be happy when my company reaches a certain pinnacle." The paradox is that the only day in which you have to be happy is today and you have to live today. I say, "Enjoy each day for all it's worth, even while you dream of a better tomorrow."

Here's another paradox: pessimism versus optimism. We want to believe and follow a leader who's optimistic, who believes he or she can win the battle. I wouldn't want to follow a leader into battle that didn't, optimistically, believe he could win. But we don't want leaders who see only optimistic results and ignore risks. How would you feel if your leader were so optimistic that he put you in harm's way because he wasn't realistic? He might be risking your life because he failed to thoroughly examine the possible consequences. An effective leader has to look at both the upside potential and the downside risk. She or he has to ask, "What would be the best-case scenario? What would be the worst case?" Having said that, I recommend to leaders that you feel more optimism than pessimism. Optimism by far outshines and outperforms pessimism. Still, you need a pessimist in every business organization. You need someone who will say, "Hey, wait a minute. Let's get real and consider this objectively. Is this great result you expect really going to happen? We are investing a lot of money into this new product, but I think there's a good chance it's not going to work."

Wright

You haven't been talking about life, have you?

Allman

Leaders are constantly challenged by paradoxes; for example, persistence versus letting go. Should you be flexible, or should you be steadfast? Should you plan for everything or be spontaneous? I favor planning, because it reduces risk. However, some people who plan their days think they have to stick with their plan even when the facts that prompted that plan have changed. They get so caught up in their picture of how things ought to be that they have removed some options. They've not learned to drop the plan when the situation changes. They can't enjoy the moment. Some days, we're better off letting our plans fly out the window. Learn to be spontaneous. Fly by your intuition. Often, that's when serendipitous events—the best successes in our lives—occur. Then, I suggest you let your experience just hang out. Let your real self rule. Of course, if you were to make that your plan for every day, you would never create the better future you want. You'd simply be reacting to other people's actions. You may never make your vision happen.

Wright

It's like a workaholic that works fifty-two weeks a year without stopping. He looks forward to retirement, when, in fact, he could retire at least once a year by simply going on vacation.

Allman

Right! That's it exactly.

Allman

From all these examples, we see that almost every success principle has its opposite. Usually, we need to apply both principles at the same time. Sometimes, we want to choose the easy way and apply half of each principle. But usually it doesn't work to compromise with a fifty-fifty formula. Half cold and half hot water usually don't work best. It is more like one time I need thirty percent of one principle, and fifty percent of the other. I have to finesse the knob back and forth until I get it right for the situation.

Wright

A minute or two ago, you mentioned leadership. Leadership is a difficult subject to define. People have their own ideas. You've written that employees will rise no higher than the example the leaders live and the principles they apply in their lives. Could you explain more what you are talking about?

Allman

Yes. I believe leadership is about results. Ultimately, everything is about the results. The measure of your leadership is the results, or the impact on your people and projects. The evaluation question is: "If you're the leader, will you get better results than if someone else were the leader?" The best results, optimal results, happen under the best leaders. Therefore, a leader's responsibility is to create results.

Results come in two categories—projects that succeed and people who synergize. Synergy happens when everyone on your team works together smoothly and cheerfully, when they blend their skills and when they build on each other instead of competing against each other. Results are the measure of a leader. Looking deeper, I've learned that leaders produce admirable results only when their characters and principles draw followers to them. A leader is someone with followers. However, not all followers produce good results. Results are best when people volunteer to follow. Just because you are the boss doesn't mean that people will follow you. You may have the company's power to demand something, but you must recognize that your employee is still a volunteer. He or she can leave your employ. In the end, you have little political power and must rely on persuasive power. One reason Saddam Hussein didn't last long after we conquered Iraq was because some of his people were volunteers. He had tried to use political power, even the barrel of the gun, to get his people to follow him. After that power dissolved, the volunteers deserted. His armies folded. I'm saying that "the speed of leader is the speed of the pack." That's an old Eskimo proverb. The emotional vitality of a business is directly related to the leader's emotional vitality. Leaders that bring out the best in employees can produce amazing results. That's why effective CEOs today are paid high salaries. That's why, when a sports team has a bad season, the owners don't fire the players; they fire the coach. When a team like the L.A. Lakers consistently produces outstanding results, you always find the coach is an inspiring leader like a Phil Jackson, a Pat Riley, a Casey Stengle, a Vince Lombardi, a Lou Holtz or a Herb Keller. Southwest Airlines, as well as G.E., had a leader that could be credited with the emotional vitality of the group. When a leader professes principles that his followers admire, when he lives and reflects the principles, when he creates an environment of respect that's conducive to peak performance, then the employees will voluntarily follow him. Thus, leadership largely works in proportion to the principles he or she uses. It's the life he or she lives. If people trust him, if they believe in him, if they like him, they will follow. They will give more than just their hands and feet but also their heads and hearts.

Wright

Many years ago in Waco, Texas, a man told me almost the same thing you just said. He stated it a little differently, but he said, "If you think you are a leader and you look behind and see no one is following you, then you're only out for a walk."

Allman

Totally true.

Wright

In your seminar "Inspiring Leadership," you talk about using trust and authority correctly. Can you give us an example?

Allman

In my seminars, what I actually teach is trust, authority and affinity. Let me explain. Picture in your mind a building. I call it the leadership building. Imagine that two pillars support the roof. The roof symbolizes leadership. The leadership roof is what covers the building and faces the world. At the bottom of the building is the foundation. The foundation of leadership is trust. Without trust, the whole building would collapse. If you were my leader, why would I follow you if I didn't trust you? If I felt like you were going to put me into harm's way, or if I felt like you were incompetent, I wouldn't follow you. Personal relationships have the same foundation. The foundation of all relationships is trust. Without honesty and trust, leadership stands on a foundation of sand. The leader has to be honest and have integrity.

Now back to our imagined building. Remember, the two pillars that hold up the leadership roof? The two pillars are affinity and authority. Affinity means liking. Authority implies respect. I believe that people want a leader whom they like and respect. First, we enjoy following people we like. Liking is a large part of affinity but not all of it. Affinity has another facet. It's called rapport. Rapport makes the relationship reciprocal, equally helpful. Rapport describes a relationship of two people, both of whom work in harmony. A great leader creates a workplace where people like him and he works well with them. In your work life, you may have known a leader you didn't like. Did you notice you were tempted to work less capably, to slow down or even sabotage him? Behind such a leader's back, people will try to sabotage him. If he fails, they will be glad. Think about this. Why didn't you see Saddam Hussein leading his troops? The fact was his troops didn't like him. If I were a general and knew my troops didn't like me, I wouldn't want the troops behind me to have guns. Saddam Hussein hadn't learned that when followers like you, they will give more than just their hands and feet.

Wright

You remind me of a man who married one of my cousins. I was living in South Carolina near Fort Jackson several years ago, and he was in his late sixties when he came out to visit. We even found the old Quonset hut where he did his training back prior to World War II. He worked for Patton, and he always said that the reason the men loved Patton so much was that they could look up and see him there with them.

Allman

That's a good example. Another general, Norman Schwartzkopf, said, "I love my troops, and they love me." Followers produce their best when they feel an emotional connection with a leader. But of course, it's not that simple. The paradox is another opposing principle—the authority principle. A leader can't be simply a likable friend. She or he must also demand respect. His followers have to regard him as an authority in his organization. An employee, a constituent, a follower judges a leader to be an authority when he believes that leader is competent, when that leader has character, when that leader knows his strengths and weaknesses and when that leader demands results. Great leaders succeed when their people not only like them but also respect them. Respected leaders are not wishy-washy. Great leaders hold their followers accountable. In my leadership class, I teach that you must make a connection with your followers, and they have got to love you. Then you use the leadership tactics to get them to perform and hold them accountable. Without accountability, you get complacency. A leader is required to turn up the heat occasionally, to become a "tension thermostat," as I call it. Great leaders get their people to take their vision seriously. After all, you are trying to lead them where you want them to go. They will vigorously follow you if they like and respect you and if they have adopted your vision as their own. When you have captured their hearts, you can hold them accountable for results by using tactics like coaching, measuring and recognizing good behavior. When you hold them accountable, they act more responsibly. Better yet, they deserve credit for success. Of course, some employees still cause problems. Much of leadership is not fun. You have to give followers feedback on their performance. Occasionally, you must coach unacceptable behavior. The ability to do that is what made Lombardi a great coach. Sometimes, his players hated him because he was a taskmaster, but the reality was they loved him because they knew that he loved them.

Wright

I am beginning to understand your paradox theory by the way.

Allman

How do you achieve both liking and respect at the same time? I'll give you an example. Suppose you were in the army and merely liked the general but didn't respect him. If he were leading you into battle and you didn't respect him because he was incompetent, you wouldn't follow him too closely. You'd say, "You go first. You go way ahead." On the other hand let's assume that you respected him but didn't like him. If I were your leader, and I knew you didn't like me, I wouldn't want to be in front, because you would be behind me and you would have a gun. You're likely to sabotage me. So before any battle, I have got to figure out a way to blend the principles— to finesse the shower knob, so to speak—to get my troops to love me while I love them while I command respect and demand accountability for results.

A while ago, I was teaching this principle to a youth group. A young man, sixteen years old, came up to me. He said, "I wish my father would learn this. You know, I hate my father, but I also really respect him, because he demands certain things out of me. I respect him as a person, but you know what? We have no relationship. He doesn't spend any time with me. I don't feel that he cares about me. I wish my father knew that he needed to do both."

So it applies to parenting as well as to leading a business. I think you see. I have got to get my children to love me, and they have got to know that I love them. But for the same reason, I have to make sure that I hold them accountable for results. I have got to teach them responsibility. I've got to teach them some of the tough lessons in life, because if I don't hold them responsible, will they act responsibly when I'm not with them? It is easy to be a leader, to get people to do what you want them to do if you pay them or if you are right there with them with a really big stick. But what do your children do when you are not there? Do they follow you then? That's when your example is paramount.

Wright

One of your topics is customer service. It seems to me that customer service has fallen to an all-time low. I have been to more seminars, listened to more tapes down through the last two or three decades on customer service than almost any other single topic. Yet customer service seems to me to be in a shambles. What do you think has gone wrong with treating people as valued customers today?

Allman

I think there are two problems—customers' higher expectations and retailers' spotty fulfillment of those expectations. The first problem is that customers' expectations have risen. Customers expect more, because some businesses have raised the bar. After customers saw how Disney World treated their guests, they would return home and expect every retailer to offer them the same royal treatment. Besides our having to jump over a higher bar, we face customers who are more sophisticated, educated and demanding than they were a few years ago. Someone has said, "The customer is no longer king. She is dictator." Furthermore, she has more power. She can expect her demands to be met, because if one store doesn't satisfy her, she'll go to another. She has a surplus of retail sources to choose from. We work in a customer's market. This is the decade of the customer.

The second reason we business owners are not serving our customers better is, I believe, that we give uneven service. Sometimes, we serve customers very well and other times we don't. Why is that? I think it's largely because we hire the wrong people for service jobs. How do the organizations around the country that are known for customer service, like Nordstrom's and Southwest Airlines, provide consistently great service? The key is they are very careful about who they hire. They hire right, and then create a culture of service. You have to do the same—find and hire people that want to serve in their hearts. It's hard—and usually impossible—for an employer to fix an employee's heart. Hiring for a good heart wouldn't be so vital if the heart didn't count for much. But I've found that the heart is more important than service techniques. In my selling classes, I tell people, "If you really care about your customer and really care about giving her the right kind of service, you can succeed, because you can learn my service techniques." From my customer service classes, they can learn techniques. However, all the techniques in the world will seem phony to the customer if the employee's heart is not right. She'll see right through him. If a salesperson is selfish and doesn't really care, that will show. The employee cannot hide it. Our customer will see the salesperson as insincere. When the heart is not right, service techniques cannot overcome the handicap. In customer service, the heart trumps everything else. Employers can't override their employees' selfishness either. They can't win customer loyalty with great products alone. Customer loyalty flows from customer service. Customers actually become loyal to a company's people, not to its products. Roughly ninety percent of customer loyalty is tied to your sales people and you. Customers are loyal to the personal relationship, and it's all about the heart.

Wright

Who or what do you think is more important in building satisfied customers—employees, products or company reputations?

Allman

This may surprise you, but I think it's all about love. To give and receive love is a basic need for all of us. Love causes our deepest emotional pains and joys. When you send someone love, you fulfill his or her basic need. About ten years ago, a study was done to determine what caused customers to leave a store in the middle of a sales pitch or to decide to switch their business to a competitor. The researchers found that most shoppers switched because they felt the salesperson or sales manager was indifferent to their concerns. In my seminars, I ask, "What is the opposite of love?" Most people say "hate," but the answer is not hate. The answer is indifference. If I hated you, at least you would be good for something. On the other hand, if I am indifferent to you, you are good for nothing. You don't matter to me. My indifference is the opposite of love, because love's core is caring.

Now that we've determined that customers leave stores mostly because they feel indifference coming from the employees, I could conclude that the best customer service is primarily about showing customers the opposite of indifference. Show them caring. In the same way, employers who want to make employees feel good must show they care. It's about sending a message of love that you care about them as people and that you care about how you treat them. All of it is about capturing the hearts of people, and it comes from love.

There are five gifts of love. The first of the five gifts of love is giving the person you love quality time. You spend focused attention with him or her. That attention includes listening and caring more about this one-on-one contact than anything else at the moment.

The second gift is what we call "words of affirmation." To give this gift, you say words that make people feel good about themselves. For one, you give them compliments. In addition, you show your love by asking permission. "May I put you on hold? Would it be okay if I took a few minutes to do this?" You are asking the customer's permission to do something for her. Whenever you use words like that, people feel they are important and that you care about them.

Of these five gifts, touch is another one. We know that when a waitress touches a male patron, she receives, on average, a thirty-seven-percent larger tip. You may notice that these gifts of love always connect you with others.

My wife's most important gift—the one she loves—is acts of service. When she wants to show love to someone, she does small things for her or him. When your salespeople use the five gifts of love, you instill loyalty in your customers and in your employees. You build a company reputation for caring.

Wright

That is very interesting. You are only the second person in my entire life who talks about apathy as it applies to relationships. I remember one man told me many years ago that as long as the husband and wife were throwing pots and pans at each other they've got hope. It is when they won't speak to each other that it's over.

Allman

Yes. Like I tell people, the first step of divorce is emotional divorce. Emotional divorce is where you pull apart and feel indifferent. You simply don't care. Caring is the bottom line. The lack of caring is happening in organizations. If the boss is indifferent to the employees, if the employees are indifferent to the customers, employees and customers tend to leave. When people are not being satisfied with customer service, they seek their satisfaction elsewhere.

Wright

Sam, with our *Mission Possible!* book we are trying to encourage our readers to live better and to be more fulfilled by listening to the examples of our guests. Is there anything or anyone in your life that has made a difference for you and helped you to become a better person?

Allman

First are my parents. I could list many lessons, but here are just a few. First, my mom taught me the power of unconditional love. She was always there, no matter how I behaved. She taught me that. My dad taught me the power of work. As a kid, you heard that I started to lay carpet when I was eight or nine years old. My dad was literally a workaholic. By that, I don't mean that he was the kind of guy that, when he heard about work, went out and got drunk. He was a workaholic who expected me to work the same long hours he did. He taught me to work. Secondly, and more importantly, he taught me the importance of integrity and honesty in my work. The best compliment anyone can give me today is that I am a "chip off the old block."

My second wife has also made a great difference in my life. When she married me, I had five children and she had two little children. We combined our families. At age twenty-six, she became the mother of seven children. I deeply admire her commitment to make it work. She is also the most unselfish person I have ever met. From her, I've learned to give. Those are deep lessons I've learned from family. In addition, I've had several teachers who believed in me and taught me about life. They guided me to do what I do. Those three or four teach-

Mission Possible!

ers influenced me to get where I am today—and quickly—because I wanted to be like them. I wanted to affect people's lives positively, like these people affected mine. They cared about me. They made me feel I could make a difference. They taught me the great lessons of life.

Wright

It's fascinating. I don't remember which survey it was, but I have tried it in workshops before. I've asked people to list the top five people who have influenced their lives. For a majority of people, the top three are teachers. I mean as far back as third and fourth grade even. It is fascinating how teachers have such a strong impact on all of our lives.

Allman

It is amazing what happens when you have someone who believes in you. Rick Patino one time said the biggest job of a leader or a parent is to get people to believe in themselves. When someone else believes in you, you become increasingly capable of great things. You are willing to make things happen.

Wright

By the way, I got that same accolade that you were talking about. I don't have ten children as you do, but I do have three. They start at forty-one, and the smallest one is fourteen.

Allman

My youngest is eight and my oldest is thirty-six.

Wright

How about that! I received a card from my forty-year-old son, who is a giant. He is six feet, five inches tall, and he is an athlete. He sent me a card recently that said, "I'm not a chip off the old block. I'm a chunk off the old ark." He's still got humor, but I took it as a real compliment.

Allman

It's all worth it when you feel like you have made an impact on someone's life.

Wright

When you talk about the people who influenced you, your mom and dad, your wife and teachers, what do you think makes a great mentor or coach? In other words, are there characteristics that mentors have in common?

Allman

Yes. First, the mentor must be respectable and likable. As I said earlier, to make me want to follow a leader or mentor, the person must be someone I respect. I respect people who walk their talk. They profess good principles and are principle centered. More importantly, they have the integrity to abide by those principles. Furthermore, I have to love, or at least like, my mentor. Third, I want a mentor who believes in me. My favorite mentors made me feel like I could do something. Fourth, they had deep personal experience. They knew about life. They were wise. They applied with me the "principles of influence" and didn't force their philosophy on me. They just taught me. In addition to all these qualities of a great mentor, the student has to be ready to learn. As they say, when the student is ready, a teacher will appear. When someone needs a mentor, they usually find one who will teach them the lesson they need at that time. Part of it is being in the right place at the right time.

Wright

This is very interesting. If you could have a platform and tell our listeners and readers something that you feel would help or encourage them, what would you say to them?

Allman

Bottom line?

Wright

Bottom line.

Allman

The purpose of life is happiness. If you are not happy and fulfilled, you are probably doing the wrong things. By "happy and fulfilled," I don't mean what happens after you become rich and retire from work. I also don't mean "pleasure" that may excite you today but bring regret or disappointment tomorrow. By "happy," I mean feeling at peace, today, with your circumstances and yourself. Feeling in harmony with your conscience and realizing you are effectively serving others.

If you want to know what brings us lasting joy—what leads us to feel happiness and fulfillment—I will share my experience. It coincides with the experience of many people before me. Happiness and fulfillment are fruits of two things—personal growth and personal meaning. This is another paradox. Happiness doesn't grow from leisure. If you want to be happy, you have to work, to grow and improve yourself. You have to become self-actualized. The reason I believe that—and this is a major part of my teaching mission—is I believe that people become happy by learning and growing. They can't ever stop doing that. Knowledge gives us power because it gives us choices. It gives us alternatives. The reason most people aren't happy is they keep doing the same thing and getting the same disappointing result. They don't realize they have another choice. If they had more knowledge, they would have alternatives. Knowledge is power, because it gives you choices and alternatives, and it allows you to do different things. So I think lasting happiness will elude you until you work on yourself, until you grow yourself in new areas, until you learn.

The paradox is that happiness is not about you. It is not about what you get in the world. Too many people imagine that happiness comes from financial security. Therefore, they devote practically all their energy to gain worldly wealth. Stephen Covey illustrates how misleading this is. He says you may climb the ladder of success but find it leaning against the wrong building. You could be professionally successful and get all the accolades of life, but you could still end up feeling hollow, unhappy, unfulfilled. The problem is that happiness is not about you. It is not about what you get; it is what you give. It is about making a dent—a good difference in the lives of others.

That's why I say the second element of happiness is personal meaning. We have no meaning if we are the meaning. To feel happy, we need to devote our passions to a meaning greater than us—a meaning greater than our own lives and a meaning that will last beyond our brief mortality. I believe we all need something greater than ourselves to which we give our passion. We need a cause that makes the best possible difference in others' lives and in our own. For me, a cause is satisfying when it has the breadth to explain the meaning of life and to guide me to help others find happiness—here and hereafter. You may choose a different cause. Your cause may satisfy you if, in some way, it makes the world better in the long term. If you don't already devote time to such a cause, I urge you to find something that's meaningful to you—something to which you can devote your life's juices and passions. When you find it and serve the cause with all your mind, strength and commitment, I believe you will see life's trials fade in importance. You may cease to feel selfish, because you realize better that your quest is to make life better for other people.

Wright

Sam, I really appreciate your being with us today on *Mission Possible!*

Allman

My pleasure.

Mission Possible!

Wright

We have been talking today with Sam Allman. When he speaks, his audience learns. Sam makes well-known principles novel and memorable, as we have found here today. He makes new ideas understandable. Sam, thank you so much for being with us.

Allman

You are welcome. I appreciate talking with you. I've appreciated the other work I've seen you do.

Wright

Thank you so much.

Sam Allman
Allman Consulting and Training
5150 Stilesboro Rd. Suite 100
Kennesaw, Georgia 30152
(888) Will-ACT or (770) 425-2142
Email: info@IwillACT.com

Chapter 5

PETER QUINONES

Peter Quinones is actively involved in sales and investing in tax lien certificates, as well as speaking. Peter is an enthusiastic member and supporter of both Toastmasters and The National Speakers Association. In the late 1980s and early 90s he traveled the country, training thousands of salespeople and market researchers. His recent projects include a book, The Dream Factory, and ventures with well known success coaches like Michele Blood and Lance Murkin.

The Interview

David E. Wright (Wright)

Peter Quinones, a professional speaker and trainer, is actively involved in sales and investing in tax lien certificates. Peter is an enthusiastic member and supporter of both Toastmasters and the National Speakers Association. In the late 1980s and early '90s, he traveled throughout the United States training thousands of sales people and market researchers. His recent projects include a book, *The Dream Factory*, and ventures with well known success coaches, such as Michelle Blood and Lance Murkin. Peter Quinones, welcome to *Mission Possible!*

Peter Quinones (Quinones)

Thank you, David. It is a pleasure to be here. Thanks for asking me to be on the program.

Wright

You're quite welcome. Lance Murkin, the author of *Kitchen Table Gold Mine*, endorsed you, saying, "If you are looking for the keys to success, do yourself a favor and get this man's material; study it, use it." How do you define success?

Quinones

First, David, I'll give you a quote from Ralph Waldo Emerson on that subject that I like. Then I'll add my own little addendum to that. He said, "To find the best in others, to leave the world a little bit better, whether by a healthy child, a garden patch, or a redeemed social condition, to know even one life has breathed easier because you have lived, this is to have succeeded." And what I would add to that is this: If you have experienced a very significant event in your own life and you share it with others, whether it is just one other person or millions of other people, and your having shared that experience with them becomes a significant experience in their lives, then you have succeeded. That, to me, is success.

Wright

I remember a man down in Texas one time told me that you don't have to jump off a fourteen-story building to experience death; you can just read about someone else doing it.

Quinones

That's a great analogy.

Wright

Peter, we all have experienced the high of attending a motivational seminar or a workshop and a short time later seen the feelings that we've had just fade away. How do you help people stay motivated so that achievement will be the result of inspired action?

Quinones

David, motivation is something that's got to be right up in your face, and it's got to be there all the time, and you have to have some devices that help you keep it there, keep you aware of it. What I do in my seminars is give out two articles to the attendees, which, I hope, communicate the importance of staying motivated every single day.

The first thing we give out is this large gold chart that lists various categories of goals and various timetables within which the person would like to meet those goals. I have a calligrapher do this. It is not something that we run off at Kinko's. We actually hand write out a certain amount of goal charts. These are very large, and we pass them out and encourage people to hang them up at home, in the bedroom or in the kitchen—wherever it is easiest for them to see them. This is something that they can look at every day and be reminded of their goals.

The second thing we give out is a painting, which has a woman's face on it and represents two states of consciousness. The first side of the painting is our outer face that we show to the world every day; the other side represents the interior psychological state that we all have, and this is a reminder that the inner has to balance with the outer. I think that in order for our goal compass to be working correctly, we have to balance our inner and outer states. So I give out these two visual aids as a reminder, hopefully, that we need to stay motivated every single day, without exception.

Wright

What do you think about the people who set and therefore do not obtain unrealistic goals? When someone who has been overweight most of his life says, "I m going to lose seventy five pounds" on January first and then doesn't, how does he live with that guilt?

Quinones

Better to try to lose five pounds first. I think your eventual goal may be to lose seventy-five, but you have to go slowly. In response to that question specifically, I think you have to reach a certain level of disgust factor with yourself when you have a situation in your life that you want to change. You have to be at the point of no return, where you are not going to tolerate it any longer.

Wright

That is interesting. In your new book, *The Dream Factory*, you refer to USP, or "unique selling proposition." Tell our listeners and our readers what you mean.

Quinones

The unique selling proposition is a critical tool, both in business and in our personal lives. This is a concept that was originated by an advertising copywriter named Rossa Reeves, and basically what it says is that this product and only this product can give you this particular benefit, and if I can, I'll give you a brief example of how Reeves himself used this with a product. M&M candies came to him in the late 1950s, when their sales were very bad and the candy wasn't selling at all. They wanted him to try to create a commercial that would help them out of that situation, so what he did was study the candy for a little while. After doing so, he knew exactly what he wanted to do. He made a TV commercial in which he put two closed fists on the screen, and the voiceover on the commercial said, "Which of these two hands is holding M&M candies?" The first hand opened up, and it was all streaked with chocolate. The second hand opened up, and it was perfectly clean, with no streaks. The voiceover says, "Not the hand that's messy, because M&Ms melt in your mouth, not in your hands." That was the unique selling proposition that Reeves found for M&Ms, and as we all know, it certainly worked.

Wright

For some other business, it might take a little innovation. The thing that keeps M&Ms from getting all over your hands is the protective coating.

Quinones

Oh, absolutely.

Wright

Could we as business people figure out what would be unique to our product or service? How difficult would that be?

Quinones

I'll give you another, more recent, example from our own time. Domino's Pizza guaranteed they would give you a hot pizza within thirty minutes or you wouldn't pay. No one else was willing to make that kind of guarantee, and as we know, that certainly worked for them.

Wright

So we just take our product or service and improve it to the point that it's unique to others.

Quinones

Absolutely.

Wright

In the fifth chapter of your book, you pose the question, "Why are you here?" Do you find that most people explore and decide their purpose in life, or do they just go along with whatever happens to them?

Quinones

My own personal experience is that most people do both of those things. I think most people do know what their hearts desire is, why they are here, what they would like to be doing in a perfect world, but unfortunately they don't act on it. They feel that it is not obtainable for them or that it is something that's beyond their reach. They are afraid of rejection. They don't have the ability. They have false beliefs such as, "You have to be born wealthy or inherit money or have the right connections." They fall in with negative people who tend to discourage ambition and, unfortunately, never act on their dreams.

Wright

So, what separates people that have a purpose is action.

Quinones

Absolutely. It is action and belief. It is the combination of the mental belief that it is possible to achieve your dream and the physical reality of putting plans to reach your dreams into concrete practice.

Wright

What do you think causes some so much self-doubt?

Quinones

Jim Browne has a saying that is very, very true, and I'm going to quote it: "It is very easy to achieve your dreams, but it is a little bit easier not to. I think that is very, very true.

Wright

It just takes more effort.

Quinones

A little more effort, yes.

Wright

I was fascinated with your discussion of teleiolack and how it affects goal setting. Could you tell us what teleiolack is?

Quinones

Yes. Way back in about 300 B.C., Aristotle articulated the concept of teleology. What that means is human beings are gold-directed creatures. We behave for a reason. We aren't like animals that just get up and graze in the fields all day. Our actions have reasons behind them. Unfortunately, what I have found is that while we can explain our individual actions we very often have trouble explaining the purpose of what our lives as a whole is. Let me give you an example. If I ask you why you brush your teeth in the morning, you'll give me an answer immediately. If I ask why you put a coat on in the winter, you can answer immediately. But if I ask, "What is the purpose of your life? What are you doing on the planet Earth? Why are you here?" most people will look at you with an amazed look. They won't be able to articulate an answer. I think that is a big hindrance.

Wright

Do you think our actions define who we are?

Quinones

Absolutely. I think that if you just get up and go to a job, and if I ask, "Why do you do this particular job? Why are you working here?" and the only reason you can give me is, "Because I have to pay my bills," then that's a problem. Your actions indicate what s going on inside your mind.

Wright

I was very interested in your comments in your book about innovation and thinking outside the box. You told a story of a truck that gets stuck under an overpass because it is too tall. You say to think outside the box. Tell us a little bit about that story and how we can apply it.

Quinones

In this particular story, the truck was a little too tall and got stuck there under the overpass. The highway department and the police were around with all of these cranes and trucks, trying to pull it out from under the bridge where it was stuck. A little boy happened to be there observing the situation, and he said to a policeman, "Why don't you just let the air out of the tires?" Which none of the adults had thought of. So when I say "think outside the box," that's what I mean. We have to literally think like children, because children don't curb their imaginations at all. They just say whatever comes to mind and try to act on it very often. I think as adults, we've fallen into a pattern where we have beliefs like, "This is the way we do things around here" or "This is the way it's always been," which prevent us from getting outside the box. There was a time when Christopher Columbus was the only person in the world that believed the earth was round. That's an example of thinking outside the box. I think it's a trait that's shared by most of the great scientists and artists in history.

Wright

I remember taking a week-long seminar on creativity several years ago, and the seminar leader had us write down how many uses we could think of for a paper clip. I thought a paper clip was to clip papers, and so when I finished, I had four or five legal pages of things that could be done with a paper clip. I was really proud of myself and all of my innovative thinking and everything. Then he said, "Okay, now write down what you can do with it if you triple its size, and you are kind of stunned by innovative thinking. Sometimes it just takes sitting there thinking about it a little bit and wondering what else could happen.

Quinones

Absolutely. That's a great example.

Wright

With our *Mission Possible!* talk show and book we are trying to encourage people in our audience to live better and to be more fulfilled by listening to the examples of our guests. Is there anything or anyone in your life that has made a difference for you and helped you to become a better person?

Quinones

Yes, absolutely. In my life, my father and my sister have been the chief influences on me. My father came here as a young man. He didn't speak the language. He joined the navy once he learned English, bought a house and had children, one of which had a severe illness at birth. He kept going and going and going. He had a very sick wife for many years, but eventually, he achieved the American dream; he achieved complete financial independence and is a very happy man now. I respect him a lot, and I wish I had listened to him when I was younger. My sister has been another great example for me. She has overcome a lot of adversities. She has earned three advanced degrees from prestigious universities and has done very well in her chosen field. They both have been my mentors and my real influences.

Wright

I m sure that we all look back and think what might have been if we had listened more, but there is a good side to that as well. If you tell enough people that you didn't listen, you might encourage them to listen a little bit better while they are younger. It might balance out.

Quinones

Aristotle begins his book *Politics* with a fifty-page discussion about families and how the family should be organized. So that's a good recommendation right there.

Wright

What do you think makes up a great mentor? In other words, are their characteristics that mentors seem to have in common?

Quinones

Absolutely. Number one, they are able to quickly spot a person who has the talent or the ability to go far, and if a mentor feels that this person is not serious or is not dedicated enough he won't waste his time with a person who is not serious. I believe that's the first characteristic. Secondly, I believe that a mentor is flexible enough to provide his own knowledge, guidance and expertise to the protégé, but at the same time, the mentor gives the protégé enough room for his own individual expression and his own individual message in whatever field he happens to be working for. I think also that most mentors have the maturity to know that if you get in the business of mentoring people, eventually some of your protégés are going to surpass you and achieve more than you achieved. But they will never forget their mentors and will always be indebted to them for their help.

Wright

Most people are fascinated with these new television shows about being a survivor. What has been the greatest comeback you have made from adversity in your career or in your life, for that matter?

Quinones

Sometimes I feel that I have had every problem a person could possibly have: money, health, relationships, weight, you name it. But I really feel I overcame adversity in a big way when I was able to quite smoking, and the way I was able to do that was by getting to a place I alluded to earlier, which was called the disgust factor. I became so disgusted. I had tried everything—the patch, the gum, cold turkey and nothing worked. So you have to get to the place where you say, "I refuse to be denied what I want now, and I'm either going to change or I'm going to die—one or the other." I think once you reach that level, whether it s a health issue like smoking or anything else, nothing is going to stop you; you are going to achieve what you want to achieve, period, the end.

Wright

When you consider the choices you have made down through the years, has faith played an important role in your life?

Quinones

Absolutely. You know, Napoleon Hill said that faith is the head chemist of the mind. That is defiantly true. You can't achieve anything if you don't believe that it's possible for you and if you don't have the faith to keep going, no matter what kind of obstacles are standing in your way. And I believe most of us that succeed or that want to succeed realize that you are going to benefit not only from your own faith but from the faith that other people have in you, people who help you and who believe that you can achieve your goals and give you assistance in going on toward them. Hill also said that the repetition of affirmation to your subconscious mind is the only know method of developing faith. I think it is very true. I place a lot of emphasis on affirmation.

Wright

I read some statistics recently about how many hours the average American watches television—mindless dribble stuff—and how much time we spend just wasting time. Somewhere in the back of your book, you have a chapter about persisting, and you say it's largely a matter of making it happen in you mind first, through visualization and affirming, then just waiting for the outcome to manifest itself in physical reality while you take your practical action steps. They would almost be mutually exclusive would they not, the person who sits around and just lethargically does nothing and that person who is persisting?

Quinones

Absolutely. They are two completely different people, and if you met them, you could tell within ten minutes who was who.

Wright

How can you move from being a lethargic person to being someone who does persist? I remember that for many years Paul Myer wrote a lot about visualization and affirmation. He took it almost to a science, and, of course, I believe in it. But how do you get others to understand that sometimes seeing is not believing and that believing is seeing?

Quinones

Let me give you an analogy, David. Some people are what I call "people who argue with the weather." Let me explain to you what I mean. If you come out of your house one day and it's pouring rain and you don't particularly want it to be raining that day—let's say you have a ballgame or a barbecue planned—and you start screaming to the sky. That's not going to help you. Similarly, if you learn that every successful person who has ever achieved anything says that you have to do visualization and you have to do affirmation, then you can't argue with that; you have to do it, period, the end. If you want to be successful to achieve your dreams and to have a worthwhile and fulfilling life, you must do visualization and affirmation. If you say otherwise or make excuses, then you re arguing with the weather. You just can't do it. I hope that answers that question.

Wright

It does. In your book you quote a lot of famous people—Ralph Waldo Emerson, Carl Young, et cetera—when you talk about the superconscious mind and you say it is the most powerful force available to you. Could you tell us a little bit about what you mean by that?

Quinones

Absolutely. I'll give you an example. I was writing my book, and I wrote, as you may recall, the first couple of chapters in the second part are about a synchronistic event that occurred to me involving a person's birthday. I had met my co-author, Janice, in a gym, and when I asked her what her birthday was, it turned out to be the same day as the person in my book. Well I tell you, I almost fell off the exercise bike. That's an example of the superconscious. And once you teach your mind how to take advantage of it and tap into it, unbelievable things start to occur to you. It's really a very powerful source.

Wright

What is a signpost event?

Quinones

A signpost event is an event that happens to you at a very early time in your life that is pointing toward future events that have not yet taken place. And you only know that it is a signpost event in retrospect, when you look back. When it occurs, you can't identify it as such at that point in time. It s only in the future, when the other events occur, that you can say, "Wow, this was pointing me in that direction." That's a signpost event.

Wright

I was really interested when I read that chapter. I took a pencil and went back in my mind and jotted down two or three signpost events. They were not only pivotal but they did literally shape the future.

Quinones

It's true. If you reflect seriously for just a few moments, you'll see that it happens.

Wright

If you could have a platform and tell our audience and our readers something you feel could help or encourage them, what would you say?

Quinones

I would ask them to close their eyes for a couple of minutes and vividly recall by means of all their senses, the most pleasant, happy event that has taken place in their lives up to this point. And recreate it vividly with sounds, colors, taste, touch, sight—all of the senses—and bring it to life in your mind in the most vivid, incredibly exuberating fashion. Recreate the feeling that you had when these happy events were taking place, and then realize that just as you can do that with something that happened in the past, you can do it with something that you want to happen in the future. Because your mind can't distinguish real time, it only knows what you tell it, so keep in mind that you can make your future successes just as real in your mind right now as your past successes. That's the key really to having a successful life.

Wright

Peter we really appreciate you being with us today on *Mission Possible!* Is your book somewhere that we can offer our listeners and readers the option to buy it?

Quinones

You can go to www.iuniverse.com. You can order it right from that web page.

Mission Possible!

Wright

We have been talking today with Peter Quinones, a professional speaker and trainer and the author of *The Dream Factory*, which I have read and would heartily endorse. It is something that will help you discover who you are and the possibility of what you might become. Peter, thank you so much for being with us today.

Quinones

Thank you, David. It's been my pleasure.

Peter Quinones
PO Box 478
Brooklyn, New York 11209
Phone: 917.941.2387
Email: pqq@compuserve.com
www.peterq.net

Chapter 6

LES BROWN

Les Brown is an internationally recognized speaker and CEO of Les Brown Enterprises, Inc. He is also the author of the highly acclaimed and successful books, Live Your Dreams *and* It's Not Over Until You Win. *Les Brown is one of the nation's leading authorities in understanding and stimulating human potential.*

The Interview

David E. Wright (Wright)

Today we're talking with Les Brown, a renowned professional speaker, author and television personality. Born in low-income Liberty City in Miami, Florida, Les and his twin brother, Wes, were adopted when they were six weeks old by Mrs. Mamie Brown, a single woman with very little education or financial means but a big heart. In grade school, he was labeled as a slow learner by teachers—a stigma that stayed with him, damaging his self-esteem for many years. With a passion to learn and a hunger to realize greatness, Les initiated a process of unending self-education that has helped him rise from a hip-talking morning DJ to broadcast manager, from community activist to community leader, from political commentator to three-term legislator and from a banquet and nightclub emcee to a premier keynote speaker. Les is the recipient of the National Speakers Association's highest honor—the Council of Peers Award of Excel-

Mission Possible!

lence. He was also selected as one of the world's top five speakers by Toastmasters International and a recipient of the Golden Gavel Award. Les Brown, welcome to *Mission Possible!*

Les Brown (Brown)

Thank you very much. It's a pleasure to be here with you to talk about a few things, David. Thank you for having me.

Wright

Les, you're recognized as one of the nation's leading authorities in understanding and stimulating human potential. How do you go about challenging people to change and realize their full potential?

Brown

I think that you first have to begin to help people to realize that what they're doing right now is only the tip of the iceberg of what's possible for them. Once you can begin to help them to see that, you then give them some goals that are beyond their comfort zones, things that will challenge them, and by stretching to achieve those goals, they'll begin to discover some things about themselves that they would not know otherwise.

Wright

Do they know that it's a stretch for them?

Brown

Yes, because you always want to have people set goals that will challenge them, that will help to bring up the deeper part of themselves that they never reach for. In order to do something you've never done, you've got to be someone you've never been. So one of the things I think is important is for them to set those high goals for themselves that will challenge them. Something Jim Rowen said that I think is very important is that he encouraged people to become millionaires—not for the sake of making the money but for what you become in the process. I think that when we set high goals for ourselves as we're stretching, reaching, trying to begin to make those things happen, we have a lot of disappointments, a lot of setbacks, a lot of failures. We fall short again and again and again. But all of those character-building experiences develop our skills, help us to fortify our faith, give us more confidence in ourselves, and we become better people because of those things that we grow through rather than just go through as we're reaching for our goals.

Wright

I know you speak to thousands each year. How do you get people who seem to have absolutely no purpose in life to realize that they need to have attainable goals?

Brown

I think that it's important when we're talking with people to first of all get to know them and find out what makes them tick. Sometimes people are not motivated, because they don't want to fail. They think about things like their past experiences, the things they've gone through, the disappointments they've had, the doors they've had shut in their faces, the things they tried to do that didn't happen, and they surrender to life. I remember a line in a book, in which a character named Bigger Thomas said, "The impulse to dream has been slowly beaten out of me through the experience of life." So there are people who, because of their conditioning, their circumstances, the things that have happened to them that just knocked the wind out of them, have begun to stop dreaming. They don't even think about dreaming anymore, because life has just been so painful, so punishing, so devastating to them. What we have to begin to do when we want to begin to reach someone like that is let them know, "Hey—you're greater than your circumstances. You're greater than anything that has ever happened to you." One of the quotes I love very much is, "When life knocks you down, try to land on your back, because if you can look up, you can get up." I think it's important for them to know, "Hey—you're not by yourself. Everybody goes through this." In fact when they want to reach some goals, it's very important for people to do several things. Among them is to realize that it's okay to fail. You don't set out to fail, but make it okay to fail. Most people allow their fear of failure to outweigh their desire to succeed. Michael Jordan has missed more shots than he's ever hit. Babe Ruth struck out more times than he hit home runs. Make it okay to fail. You're going to fail your way to success. What we do in our educational process is make people afraid of failing. Failing is a stigma; it's negative. But you want to begin to realize that that's how you learn. I remember when I was a state legislator, when I won a debate arguing for legislation that I felt strongly about. I won a debate based upon what I knew, but when I lost, I lost because of what I didn't know. That sent me back to the drawing board. So you want to make losing an educational process.

Wright

Les, I remember your first book, *Live Your Dreams*. It was really a great book. I enjoyed reading it, and it was a best seller. Tell us a little bit about your latest book, *It's Not Over Until You Win*.

Brown

I think that when they hear that title, people think in terms of winning, always coming in number one, always being on top, always reaching your goals. What I mean is that you've got to conquer that inner voice within yourself as you look at yourself, look at the goals, look at the things that you want to do. There's an old African proverb that says, "The enemy outside can do us no harm unless the enemy within cooperates." What we have to do is begin to realize that the external things that happen to us really aren't the things that shut us down, that stop us. The thing that really stops us dead in our tracks is that little voice within that says, "I can't do this. I don't have what it takes. I don't know if I can hang on any longer." That inner voice is what we have to always be aware of and monitor, because that determines our success or our failure in life. That determines whether we throw in the towel on ourselves, on our dreams, on our families and walk away or if we just start to dig in and come back again and again and again to continue to pursue the things that we want to do that give our lives a sense of value and meaning.

Wright

I read something that interested me in an article that you wrote. I think you wrote it last year. It was published in the *Messages From*

Masters series. Let me read it to you. "When you decide to move your life to the next level of accomplishment, you must fasten your mental and spiritual seatbelts. You must endure the turbulence of change before you grow." You're one of the few people I know who doesn't sugarcoat the difficulty of goal setting. Is that one of the reasons why you're so successful teaching people?

Brown

Yes. I think you have to say to people, "You're going to get hurt. You're going to fail. You're going to have some disappointments. You're going to get knocked out. You're going to get knots on your head." But that's how we grow. Don't take it personally. Don't ask, "Why did this have to happen to me?" Why not you? Who would you suggest? Do you want to give us some friends? Victor Frankel calls it "unavoidable suffering," which we'll all experience in life. Once people know that they're going to get hurt, they're going to face some moments when they're going to question themselves and doubt whether or not they can do it, when they will not be able to see the light at the end of the tunnel, then they're going to want to turn around and go back. That's all a part of the process. In spite of that, what you've got to do is hold on. Eventually, that which you are pursuing will begin to release its sequence to you. It will begin to introduce you to parts of yourself that you would never have discovered otherwise. All of us will go through what Joseph Campbell called "the long, dark journey of the soul." But as you hold on through persistence and perseverance and prayer and determination, eventually daybreak will come, and you'll realize that everything you've gone through was worth it.

Wright

I was in a Sunday school class a few months ago and heard my wife say something that I thought I would never hear her say as long as I lived. She almost died of cancer, and she told the group of people there that while she, of course, didn't want cancer, she wouldn't have given anything for the experience.

Brown

Yes, because as a four-year, six-month cancer conqueror, I feel the same way. There's a quote I love very much that says, "Many times, when the very foundation of our life has been shaken, when we have a teeth-rattling experience and go through fear and desperation, we run to God, only to discover that it's God that's doing the shaking." That's some strong stuff up there! All of these things that we are growing through bring us back to Him. I think that as we begin to know everything that's happening to us, that the universe is unfolding as it should, we should, in all things, give thanks, in glory and tribulation. As you begin to realize that adversity introduces you to yourself and you receive that adversity and go through that pain and suffering and you see it as a gift, then life takes on a whole new meaning for you.

Wright

I want to ask you about something you wrote in another article that was published recently. You said there are three kinds of people—winners, losers and potential winners. You went on to say, "Wayward winners are not lost souls. They just need a little tweaking to get them back on course." You really give people a break, don't you, Les?

Brown

I believe that there are winners who have not discovered how to win. These people have a restlessness within them. They go from job to job. They're always seeking. They're always searching. They never give up. They're trying to find their place in the sun. There's a saying I love very much: "Man was not born to work for a living but to live his making, and living his making will make his living." There are people who have decided, "What I'm doing is not my making. It's not who I am, and I've got to be in alignment with something that I'm doing that gives my life a sense of meaning and value that can help me begin to go to the next level." Part of the process of discovering that is knowing what you value. You've got to know what's important to you. What are you willing to give up in order to make that happen?

Wright

I remember your nationally-syndicated TV talk show. On the program, you always said you wanted to focus on solutions rather than problems. Was it tough to get your message across on television?

Brown

Because of the limited time segments they gave us it was, but we established a process that Oprah Winfrey went on to adopt. When I came into television, the belief was that you could only have a show that was successful if that show were built around conflict and controversy, like the *Jerry Springer Show*. We felt that you can focus on the positive things of life and still get ratings, and we proved that. My ratings were very high the first rating period that we had. It was cancelled in spite of that, because we wouldn't play the other game. I believe that television is a very strong medium. What you focus on the longest becomes the strongest. I think we need to look into the future and look at the level of consciousness as it relates to our children and the state of mind of our country at this point in time. Focusing on the highest and best that's in us has a great deal of value in helping us begin to have a vision of ourselves and a future that's not perverted, that's not blurred with all the negative things that are coming out of television right now. It's a powerful medium to entertain people, but it also can be used to empower people. I think that's what Oprah's doing with her program now—focusing on things that can give us the methods, the tools and the commonsense things that are not common practice but can help us get some breakthroughs in our lives.

Wright

She's turning people on to reading, isn't she?

Brown

Yes, and that's very important. Oliver Wendell Holmes said, "Once a man or woman's mind is expanded with an idea or concept, it can never be satisfied to going back to where it was." That's what my work has been about as a speaker, as a trainer, in the books and on tapes—helping people to stretch their minds, helping people to live out of their imaginations as opposed to living out of their memories.

Mission Possible!

Wright

I remember several years ago, before your television talk show, when you did some powerful programs for PBS that were almost like commercials. Do you remember those?

Brown

Oh yes. We did several PBS specials—about five of them—that they used for the purpose of getting people to sign up to be members of the PBS audience.

Wright

A lot of my friends knew that I dealt with speakers on occasion, and they were asking me, "Who is this guy?" You made an impact. I kept saying, "I don't know who it is." And then I saw one of the specials. My goodness, they were powerful.

Brown

Thank you very much.

Wright

Les, with our *Mission Possible!* talk show and book we're trying to encourage people in our audience to live better and be more fulfilled by listening to the examples of our guests. Is there anything or anyone in your life that has made a difference for you and helped you become a better person?

Brown

My mother. I'm adopted. I was born in an abandoned building on a floor with a twin brother in a poor section of Miami, Florida, called Liberty City. When we were six weeks old, we were adopted. I feel like Abraham Lincoln, who said, "All that I am and all that I ever hope to be I owe to my mother." In fact, when I had a talk show, I would always end it, as I do my speeches, by saying, "This has been Mrs. Mamie Brown's baby boy." I saw a card one time I'll never forget that said, "God took me out of my biological mother's womb and placed me in the heart of my adopted mother." So my mother has been a driving force in my life to help me to do things that I don't think I would have been able to do otherwise. My goal and objective in everything I did was to make my mother proud of me. And I did make my mother proud. I wanted to buy her a home, and I wanted to take care of her. I took care of her until she passed six years ago. At this stage of my life, my goals are to help raise funds for breast cancer research, to help provide funding for research and development in the area, to reduce the number of women who die from breast cancer and to do that all in the name and memory of my mother. That's been a driving force in my life—the role of my mother in my life.

Wright

When I went to your Web site, lesbrown.com, it opened up with this great streaming video of snippets from several of your speeches. The main thing that stuck with me was what you said about your mother at the end. By the way, is your brother still living?

Brown

Yes. In fact, my twin brother and I will be working to do some projects this summer, working with kids. We'll be teaching them how to develop a sense of purpose and direction with their lives as well as the value of developing and expanding their minds through reading. We'll teach them to be conscious of their personal appearances, because you really make a statement about yourself by how you dress. We'll also be helping them to see the value of developing their communication skills. I had a high school teacher, Mr. Leroy Washington, who said to me, "Mr. Brown, develop your mind and develop your communication skills, because once you open your mouth, you tell the world who you are."

Wright

What do you think makes up a great mentor? In other words, are there characteristics that mentors seem to have in common?

Brown

I think that they have to be the message that they bring. Mr. Washington held himself to high standards. I think that mentors have to care about people and not just have good, strong character and be good examples, as Mr. Washington was. As Zig Ziglar said,

"People don't care how much you know until they know how much you care." So I think that mentors have to really care and take the time to get to know the people they want to mentor. They need to find out what drives them, what motivates them and what inspires them. How should they hold people accountable? I also think that mentors have to be competent in some area that you have an interest in and in which they can provide some coaching for you. They have to be sensitive. They have to be willing to give you some room to grow, and they must be very skillful in their language approach and how they deal with you when you fall short. What we say to people when they respect us and believe in us and hold us in high esteem can be very devastating if it's not done in a proper way.

Wright

When you consider the choices that you've made down through the years, has faith played an important role in your life?

Brown

Without any question. I think you start out thinking that you're tough and that you can do it all yourself. Ultimately, when you really look at life in the quietness of the evening, and you're lying in bed looking at the ceiling when you can't go to sleep, you realize that you've come this far by grace. You realize that everything you've done, everything you've achieved is only by God's grace and mercy.

Wright

I remember having a conversation with you several years ago. My wife was fighting cancer, and you shared that thought with me, probably because you were going through the same thing. I remember that rather than being depressed, the first thing I did was hold a prayer service the next with a group of people. They all prayed for you that night. You probably didn't know it, but they did.

Brown

That's why I'm still here. You all keep on!

Wright

I used to get calls from people all over the world, telling me, "David, our church of 3,000 prayed for your wife yesterday." It's powerful stuff!

Brown

It's been proven scientifically that prayer does work. I encourage people to pray for others, and most certainly, do put me on your prayer list! I'm going through a challenge right now, and there's something I believe very strongly in: "No test, no testimony." My PSA numbers have increased, the doctors say—and notice how I'm watching my language, because "Thou shalt decree a thing, and it shall be established unto you." They say that my PSA has increased to thirteen, and my whole thing is that you listen to what doctors say, but a friend of mine called me and said, "Don't play the numbers game." She said, "They gave their diagnosis, but God determines the prognosis." One of the things that I like to say to people who are trying to achieve goals is that I don't care who you are and what you've done, how much you've achieved and how much you've earned. But this is something I think that's very important. Ask for help, not because you're weak but because you want to remain strong. Ask for help, and don't stop until you get it. A lot of people won't ask for help because of pride. Pride cometh before a fall because of ego, and ego means Edging God Out. All of us will have our moments in the Garden of Gethsemane.

Wright

Those are great words. Most people are fascinated with the TV shows about being a survivor. What's been the greatest comeback you've made from adversity in your career or life? Is it cancer, or has there been something else?

Brown

I think my greatest comeback was the fact that I was able to still be in my right mind when my mother took her last breath. My brother and I, when we were kids, used to say that we wanted to die before Mama, because we didn't think that we could stand it if Mama died. We couldn't handle the pain. It was the most challenging experience. I'd never seen anyone die, and my brothers and sisters were all there, and we held her hand as she took her last breath. A tear came out of her left eye that was like a tear of release. Death is a beautiful thing to witness. I never thought I would ever say that, but it was an empowering spiritual experience that I will never ever forget.

Wright

If you could have a platform to tell our audience something that you feel would help or encourage them, what would you say?

Brown

I would say to them that you are more powerful than you realize and that you owe it to yourself to challenge yourself to live life and give it everything you have. Find ways in which you can make your life valuable to others as well as ways to serve others. Do the best that you can, and leave the rest to a power greater than yourself.

Wright

Those are great words. This has been the fastest thirty minutes of my life, Les. Today, we have been talking with Les Brown, a renowned professional speaker, author, television personality and, as you have all learned, a great motivator. Les, thank you so much for being on our program today.

Brown

Thank you so much. This has been Mrs. Mamie Brown's baby boy. It's been a plum pleasing pleasure as well as a privilege.

Les Brown Enterprises
8700 North 2nd Street, Suite 205
Brighton, Michigan 48116
Phone: 800.733.4226
Email: speak@lesbrown.com
www.lesbrown.com

Chapter 7

GREGORY J. MACIOLEK

Greg Maciolek has been focusing on the human side of management for over twenty-seven years. He held senior executive positions for over fourteen years and preaches what he practiced. Greg's focus is on the loss of worker productivity through mismanagement by managers and owners. He specializes in organizational problem solving by working with owners and senior executives to ensure organizational alignment and growth and by creating a culture for excellence. Greg delivers executive management programs that increase productivity throughout the organization. He also endorses and promotes the use of assessments for the hiring and development of all employees in a company.

The Interview

David E. Wright (Wright)

We are talking today with Gregory J. Maciolek, author, speaker consultant, trainer and owner of Integrated Management Resources, Inc. Uniquely, his company approaches organizational health and integrity in a holistic manner. Greg has a bachelor's degree in management and a master's degree in human resources management. He is a member of the National Speakers Association and is the current president of the National Speakers Association Tennessee chapter. He is the membership chair of the Smoky Mountain chapter of the American Society of Training and Development and adjunct instructor at the University of Tennessee's Professional and Personal Development Center. Gregory Maciolek, welcome to *Mission Possible!*

Gregory Maciolek (Maciolek)
Glad to be here, David.

Wright
Greg, I was interested in something you wrote about leadership, and I'd like to quote you here. You wrote, "What I learned over the years was that top leadership of an organization creates the culture that becomes the value system for the company." Can you tell us what you mean?

Maciolek
Sure, David. The leader of a company, whether it's a small business, large business or even a military organization, as I was involved in, sets the standards by which others in the organization follow. The employee looks to the leader's ethics, his emphasis on customer service and the quality of the product or service he provides. How does he treat his employees? Does he seek their input and treat them with respect? Or is it with disdain, treating employees as though they're just cogs in a wheel? Can employees be replaced at a whim? Does the leader make promises that he has no intentions of keeping? What's interesting about it is that leaders do this, either knowingly or unknowingly. Sometimes they don't even realize the impact that they have on an organization. Again, what's always interesting is the leader is supposed to establish the vision, the value and the mission and share all that with the people. Oftentimes, they're doing that haphazardly or they're doing it unwittingly. Sometimes they have a very good effect, and a lot of times they have a very negative effect, and they don't even realize they're doing it. They set that tone.

Wright

In the recent past, with all the integrity and honesty problems that American corporations have had, this would have really come to fore, and all these companies are suffering because of their management. Is that what you're talking about?

Maciolek

That's exactly right, and what's sad is that a lot of innocent people suffered because of those leadership lapses. I don't want to name companies, but you know all the stuff that's in the paper today with companies collapsing. Some companies have been very reputable, large companies, and because of leadership lapses or their "do as I say, not as I do" attitude, many leaders have unwittingly caused many, many innocent people to suffer as companies just came apart and went away. That's exactly what I'm talking about. Think of the culture of a company, something even as basic as, "Do we start meetings on time?" A lot of people say, "Well, I always get here at ten after nine because I know we don't start until fifteen minutes after, because that's when the boss shows up." Again, it's an attitude. What effect are they having on even simple things like what time meetings start? It's very pervasive, and the leaders make the difference. They set the tone, whether they want to or not or whether they knowingly do it or not.

Wright

I've published quite a few books about holistic medicine but have not seen it applied to corporate language. Can you explain how you work with companies from a holistic viewpoint?

Maciolek

To me, it's a medical metaphor. You don't just go into your doctor and say, "I don't feel good. How about writing me a prescription for antibiotics?" What's the doctor going to do? Just write out a prescription for you? I don't think so. He starts asking questions, right? How are you feeling? What are your symptoms? And so forth. The old axiom is, "Prescription without diagnosis is malpractice." So I approach companies by asking questions. You need to do a diagnosis. I

Mission Possible!

believe in organizational assessments. We give companies physicals. We try to get a snapshot or x-ray, so to speak, of the current status of the company through our assessment process so we can diagnosis where the problems are and start working on them.

It's not unusual for an owner to call me and say, "Do you do team building?" I'll ask, "Why do you think you need team building?" They say, "Well, morale is really low, and I want to do something fun. I read about going on a ropes course or one of these outbound experiences." They want to do it on a Saturday. They want to take their people away from their families on Saturday, and they want to go out and do a ropes course. Then they want to do trust falls because trust isn't very strong in their company. Then they want to finish up with holding hands around the fire singing "Kumbaya." Then, they think on Monday everyone's going to come to work feeling really good about themselves.

Remember, poor morale is not a symptom but a *result*, just like poor customer service is a result. What's causing poor morale? What's causing poor customer service? That's what you have to fix. Unless you approach those kinds of things holistically, you just can't go do team building or just do communications training or something like that, because that may not be what's required. If you have some real basic fundamental problem with the company, that's what you have to fix, because when you fix that, that addresses the morale problem. When you take away that irritant, morale tends to improve. That's why we approach it with a medical model: Diagnose the problem, identify underlying causes, prioritize them and then prescribe possible remedies or courses of action for the top priority item. Most of the time, owners work on fixing the easiest and cheapest problems. But that doesn't have much of an impact. Cause and effect works here. If you work on the top problem, it will in fact solve several other problems. And team building is really a by-product of the team solving real problems that affect them.

Wright

I can remember one company that decided they were going to get their wives and husbands together and have these marriage encounter weekends. They checked with the spouses at home and the reaction they got was, "If you wouldn't make Henry work on Saturday, he could come home and go to soccer games with Susie, and maybe we could get romantic on Friday nights." I understand what you're talking about. Most training that I have conducted in a corporate setting was not enthusiastically attended by the people at the top. If you are charged with the task of changing a company, do you start at the top?

Maciolek

I definitely want to do that. It's amazing how sometimes you've got to fight the leadership to get them to understand that. They want you to go "fix" their people. My wife's experience is a perfect example. She's a nurse at a large hospital, and they spent an entire year doing team building, only with the nurses and other related job categories. None of the supervisors went through the training, and none of the leadership went through the training. Guess what? Nothing changed. What it does is make people cynical, because they've been here before, they've seen it happen. I don't know if you've ever heard of BOHICA. It's an acronym that we used at Ford and other places. It means, "Bend over, here it comes again." They've seen it all before, and they know that as long as they just pay lip service for about three months, it will go away. So if you're going to change a company—and remember that we already talked about the effect the leadership has on the culture of a company—we want to make changes that are going to be institutionalized and long lasting. You've got to start with the top people. They've got to start, to use an old cliché, "walking the talk" and showing the effect of the changes on the leadership team. Then when we start bringing it down into the company, the first and second levels of supervision and the workers themselves, it's more likely to be understood and accepted by everyone.

Wright

I've always found that when the company management team sends the troops to a workshop to get something fixed or to learn anything, it would have been better had they just done nothing, because now the troops know how uninvolved and unintelligent their management team really is.

Maciolek

You're right on, David. It is amazing. I facilitate a five-day seminar that I have taught for twenty years. In some cases, I'll get owners and senior execs to attend, but other companies will only send their middle managers, because the owners think they need to "fix" them. Invariably, those who attend usually say two things. One is, "I wish I had this ten years ago," and secondly, "How do I get my boss to come to this training?" They see in themselves the need to improve, but then they say, "Why isn't my boss here? If this is so important and the company is spending good bucks to send me here, why isn't my boss here? He needs this even more than I do, because if he did this, it would be so much easier on me to do my job."

Wright

It's like going to a marriage counselor without your wife.

Maciolek

Right. Even though people recommend it, what good is it going to do you if only one side is talking?

Wright

When you assess management in a company, do you find that they clearly understand the company's goals and have a good idea of how those goals will be accomplished?

Maciolek

That's an interesting phenomenon. When I start to work with a new company, or even before I decide to work with them, I want to talk to the executive team and I want to talk to them individually. I ask them questions like, "What are the goals of the company? Where is it going? What's its health? What are its mission and values? What is the level of trust in the company on the executive team?" —all those things that you would want to know to determine where this company is currently. I'll tell you, David, most of the time, I get five or six different answers. Think about this. If you're down there at the bottom, looking up, and these people on the executive team can't figure out what's going on, how do we expect the employees to do that? How do we expect first- and second-level supervision to make decisions and the workers to make decisions that are going to be in alignment with the mission and values of the company when even the senior leaders can't figure out what the heck they are about? What's even worse is when they've got all these nice words on the walls but you don't see the words in action. That's just as incongruent and it's just as bad for the company.

Wright

I'm always fascinated by a company's mission statement. You can go through the management team and maybe three or four of them remember they had a meeting and wrote that out one day.

Maciolek

It's just like strategic planning. They attend a weekend retreat and write the strategic plan. Funny thing, though, is that strategic plans usually have a shelf life of about two weeks. Then they say, "Oh yeah—we did that." But they haven't even paid attention to it. That's why I don't talk about strategic planning as much as strategic problem solving. A company should wear their strategic hat at least one day a month and do strategic problem solving. Otherwise, they end up spending all their time on the here and how, the present, the operational and tactical stuff. That results in their continuous backing up to the strategic cliff. They go all the way back, and all of a sudden they're ready to fall off the cliff. That could mean competition is eating them alive, that they haven't been paying attention to new processes and other strategic threats. They've been backing up for about three or four years, and all of a sudden they're in trouble and they want to bring a consultant in to turn them around in ninety days. You can't do that. You've wasted all that time not paying attention strategically, doing strategic problem solving. The reason for that is that many owners tend to want to play with what's going on instead of doing the big picture stuff. Where are we going in the future? Are we putting enough into research? Are we capitalizing enough on new equipment and processes to stay ahead of the competition? Because they're not doing that, they get blindsided, and then they say, "Gee, what happened?" As I work with companies and owners, I find that some of the owners are not "big picture" people. They can't think strategically. They need to add a COO or an executive vice-president who can.

Wright

I was surprised when I read that a couple of surveys that you had read pointed to the fact that most hiring decisions are made in the first five minutes of an interview and that an interview is only about fourteen percent effective in hiring people. You went on to say that anyone could stand on a street corner, hire every seventh person and have just as much luck. That's a scary thought, isn't it?

Maciolek

It's very scary. This gets pretty involved. When the survey says that people hire in the first five minutes, they're basically going on their first impressions, things like a handshake, eye contact, grooming. They might be impressed that the applicant was on time for the interview. They equate that with a good work ethic, when this might have been the first time the applicant was ever on time in her life. We have a tendency, if you're not a trained interviewer, to also hire people who are like yourself, which may or may not be what you need for the job. I'm a very outgoing person, so I like people I can interact with. If I'm not paying attention to that and I have a very introverted candidate sitting in front of me, a person who's quiet or scared of interviews, he may not open up. Automatically, I might dismiss him. But if I'm hiring for an accounting clerk I don't necessarily want a chatty Cathy or a talkative Tommy, right? That's not what I need. If I'm not cognizant of that, it gets scary. Interviews by themselves only see the tip of the iceberg. It's only what you see and feel and what's on the application. Of course, resumes are *so* trustworthy, as we've seen in the last few years with football coaches. Remember we went through this just recently with football coaches who enhanced their resumes. Some reporters did some investigating and found out that there were several misrepresentations. It resulted in coaches losing their jobs for ethics.

Wright

I read some statistics recently about interviewing. I'm hiring several people into our company even now, so I've been reading some articles on techniques of interviewing. One of the things that really surprised me is the survey that set up a video camera and audio on interviews with a major company. They found that the person interviewing the new hires spoke ninety percent of the time and the interviewee ten percent of the time. What's that all about?

Maciolek

That's just like a salesman that talks too much. You want the buyer talking, just like you want the applicant talking. Again, I think it goes back to the fact that people aren't trained how to interview. To me, the hiring process starts with finding out exactly what the job requires. That's analyzing the skill sets, in addition to what experience they need. Do the applicants need professional credentials? If you're hiring nurses, they've got to have credentials. If you're hiring teachers, they've got to have credentials. There might be some certifications for engineering jobs and things like that. So you would want to know, objectively, what are the skill sets you're looking for. Then you also want to look at what works on the job and in your company, whether it's selling skills or customer service or personal skills. Are you leading people? Are you managing processes? Those are different kinds of things that require different kinds of skills. The other thing you want to look at is what kind of cognitive skills does the job require? By "cognitive" I mean the applicant's ability with words and numbers and her ability to reason. Is this a job where she has to use a lot of numbers? Does she have to have a lot of verbal interaction with people? How fast does she learn? It's ironic that companies end up promoting the wrong people, people they've known for a long time. They take the best whatevers—the best salesmen, the best engineers—and they make them the managers, thinking they're going to transfer those skills into managing people. But managing requires a different skill set. That doesn't mean that a very good salesman can't be a very good sales manager, but normally, top sales people don't excel at both skill sets. Sometimes the middle-of-the-road salesperson makes a better sales manager. A company thinks it's rewarding that good salesman by making him the sales manager, and it winds up punishing him. They take away his commissions, and they make him focus on managing others rather than on selling, which is what he loves to do, by the way. So management makes another dumb decision, and sometimes they'll lose that best salesperson because he's not selling anymore—the very thing he *loves* to do!

Wright

That sounds like the old Peter Principle.

Maciolek

Sure does. This is where the strength of the Profile XT comes into play. This is an assessment tool that I use with most of my clients. Since the Profile XT measures the cognitive abilities, or thinking styles, it provides the user of the report with a Learning Index. The Learning Index is a measure of expected learning, reasoning and problem solving potential. In other words, David, the higher the cognitive abilities, the more creative a person is, the better problem solver she is. She's better at handling multiple tasks and can handle chaos better. The person also learns jobs faster and works on her own better. An interesting footnote to that is that people who have lower cognitive abilities can act like they have higher abilities if they have been in a job for a long time. That's where management is misled, when they promote someone who *looks* like he is more capable than he is. Within his present position, he can handle anything because he has been at it so long. Move him to a higher position and he again has a steep learning curve. He gets frustrated, as does management, with the individual's lack of progress. Management has once again set up someone to fail.

Wright

I think I'm beginning to understand what you wrote. If you hire a good person into an unhealthy company he or she will leave at the first opportunity. How does management hire good people and keep them?

Maciolek

I think it's all part of the our holistic approach. First of all, you've got to have a healthy company. That goes back to, "Are you organizationally aligned and healthy? Are your processes in place to have a growing company? Are you hiring the right people to begin with? Is the culture that you've created through your leadership a culture where people will come to work and be challenged to excel? Will their input be listened to?" All of it is important. Companies normally run ads to get applicants. I don't know if you ever look at Sunday ads. I do, because I'm very involved in the hiring process. When I look at Sunday ads, most of them deal with wages and benefits, free meals, vacation time. If you know anything about Maslow's Hierarchy of Needs, those are lower-level needs. Basic security needs are lower level needs. I challenge companies with this: "If you're writing ads, why don't you relate the three reasons why you stay here?" If you're in a job you love and you're recognized and appreciated and you work hard and self-actualize, it takes a lot to lure you away from that company. One of the things I challenge companies with is, "Did you know that some of your people work harder for free after work than they work for you for money." They look at me as if to say, "What the heck are you talking about?" Think about people who do volunteer work, whether they volunteer at their churches, soccer leagues, the lodge, whatever. They work harder on Saturdays, Sundays and after work than they ever work for you. Why? They have status, they're appreciated, they're making a difference, and people come to them because they have information. These are the very things that you can actually provide the people at work with. These very important motivating goal objects are free, by the way, but no one seems to think they're important. All the leaders think that people work for is the dollar, and believe me, it's so much more than that. When leaders don't understand the motivational processes of individuals, they miss the very essence of why people are happy, satisfied and committed at work. If

Mission Possible!

you can get workers to that point, it takes a lot to move them out of the company.

Wright

I've always heard and read that a person is never motivated by anything tangible; it has to be intangible. And money is tangible.

Maciolek

It's really intrinsic, yes. I always say, "Without a gun or a big knife, I really can't make you do anything." At work it's interesting that people will say, "You can make people do things at work." Well, right; they're not stupid. They need to pay their bills and need to provide for their families. But what most managers fail to realize is that when employees are first hired, they come to work excited. They want to give you 110 percent. They have all these good ideas. They're overflowing with creativity. And what do managers do? They dumb them down. They say, "Look, you're paid to work. I'm paid to think. If we want your ideas we'll ask you for them." What happens is after a while, people check their brains at the door, because no one wants their input anymore. To me, the biggest waste of resources at work is the *human resource*. This is one of the largest costs of a company, by the way, and we waste the creative juices of the very people that make a company unique and better than the competition. We tend to ignore them because *they're the workers*.

Wright

Let me ask you two questions. Do you have a formula that you can share with our readers that will help them cover all the bases when they decide to hire? And, as a part of that, do you advocate using hiring assessments?

Maciolek

I started off with the ads, because I think ads are important. However, whether companies use headhunters, agencies, the Internet or their web sites, it doesn't matter; they make the same mistakes. Employers will say, "The people that answer my ads aren't what I really need." Number one, the ads are poorly written. Number two, just like

Gregory J. Maciolek

people badmouth products, employees can badmouth companies. If they don't feel very good at work and they're sitting around having beverages and pizza at the local pizza parlor, they're saying, "I'm looking for a job. I'm not satisfied. They treat me very poorly." Others will say, "I was thinking of applying for a job there, but I don't think I'm going to do that." That's all part of the process. I think having a good culture and having a good strong company are important, searching for employees that will enhance the company and not settling for "This is the best I can find."

And then I'm a firm believer in pre-employment assessment. There's always the discussion that it's not legal. The U.S. government is the biggest user of assessments. When I joined the military, I had to take assessment tests to see if I qualified for pilot training. I use assessments from Profiles International. The number one reason I do that is because they're on the Internet. They give me instant results, and they provide me with customized benchmarks. Most assessments that are out there for hiring measure only with personality or behaviors. That's fine, and that's part of the equation. But the strength of the Profile XT assessment is that it measures the cognitive ability along with occupational interests. What's important about that is I need to know the thinking styles and the learning styles of the people that are going to work for me. If I'm hiring, for instance, production workers or call center operators who like routine jobs, who like to do their jobs and go home, there are people who fit that mold. If I need managers or people who can handle chaos, who are problem solvers and creative thinkers, I need to have people who learn quickly and are higher on the cognitive scale. That answers the question, "Can they do the job?"

The second question is "Will they like doing that kind of work?" For instance, I'm really good with numbers. Now let me tell you, you couldn't put me in an accounting job and let me work numbers all day. That's not where I am; that's not what I love to do. Not only do I want to hire somebody who has the ability to do the job, I want them to have a desire to do that job. If I'm hiring bank tellers, I want to have people who are attentive to detail, who like doing that kind of stuff so that I'm not spending an hour every day after work helping them balance their tills. Then, of course, you take the behavioral traits in making sure that they fit the job. Hiring assessments are about one third of the hiring decision. You do recruiting, you look at resumes and applications, you do a preliminary telephone screen, and every one of those things knocks people out. Then I would do a hiring assessment before I do major interviewing. The reason is I want to know if they're going to fit what I'm looking for.

Wright

You're serious about the hiring process.

Maciolek

Absolutely, and to me it's just like fighting a war. The more you plan, the easier it is to execute any kind of plan. People dismiss the hiring process as a necessary evil, when in reality, it's one of the most important things that is going to help their companies. Turnover cost is thirty to forty percent of an annual salary. That's a conservative number. If you're hiring at higher levels or you're hiring salespeople, it can be two or three times that person's annual salary. Only a few, progressive companies track turnover cost as a line item in the budget. I've actually run into some companies in the last year or so that knew what their turnover rate was and what their cost of turnover was. I'm amazed, because when you start looking at it, it's scary.

My best example is a law firm I worked with. They were part of a nationwide law firm. They went back nine years and looked at turnover of their attorneys. They calculated conservatively that over nine years it costs them $36 million in turnover costs, and that was a conservative number. Interestingly enough, that was their net profit for the year before. That's a pretty big number. Now that you've got these candidates in front of you, you really need to do a very good job of interviewing them. I really like multiple interviews and even interviews where you have two or three people asking questions. I want to see if the applicant answers consistently. I want to get input from a variety of interviews. And the supervisor of this position should always be involved in the hiring process. That gives him or her ownership if this person is hired. I think it's really key.

Wright

Let's change the subject for a minute. How much of your practical management skills did you receive in the military? I understand you were a pilot. Did pilot training help establish any management techniques?

Maciolek

Going to pilot training when I was twenty-three years old had a profound effect on my life. Pilot training in the United States Air Force is fifty-two weeks of grueling challenges. Thirty percent, on average, wash out of pilot training for various reasons. Some wash out for medical reasons, but most are for flying deficiencies. You're flying high performance airplanes, and in the last five months of pilot training you're flying supersonic trainers that go Mach 1.4. You're leading four ships in formation, much like you see the Thunderbirds doing. You do that kind of flying in pilot training. It was the best confidence builder for me that I ever had. I was always successful in high school. I was the class president, played sports and things like that, but when I came out of pilot training, I felt I could do almost anything. It caused me to be disciplined. It caused me to be organized and focused on what I had to do. Let me tell you, when you're leading a four-ship formation through the weather, there's an awful lot of things that are going through your mind as the flight leader—to be sure that you come out of the weather safely and get your team safely to their destination. In combat, flying is second nature, because you're busy employing the weapons systems of the airplane. I was an interceptor pilot, so our unit was chasing Russian bombers along the east coast and intercepting unknown targets, like drug runners. You may be down to 500 feet, you're working the radar, you're talking on the radio, you are trying to fly the airplane. Talk about multitasking! All of that's going on at the same time. You really need to pay attention. That year of pilot training and the subsequent flying I did had a profound effect on me.

I became a flying commander and was responsible for 1,100 people of a flying group in Michigan, sitting on twenty-four-hour alert. When you have a flying group, you have not only pilots and maintenance people but you have cooks, civil engineers, doctors, nurses, supply. You're running a little city. I was responsible for twenty-four F-4s, then twenty-four F-16s, a half-billion dollars in assets and a thirty to forty million dollar budget in the late '80s and early '90s. You find out that you can't do everything. What really focuses you is that you have a mission to do. And you as the leader have an impact on how the mission will be executed. You depend on your people. I had four deputies, thirteen squadron commanders, and I needed to work through them. There was no way I could know what was going on with 1,100 people at any one time. My philosophy has always been to push decision making down to the lowest level—to make the people on the line responsible for themselves, to make the right decisions without having to go ask "Mother, may I?" They knew what needed to be done, and I was rarely disappointed in the actions of my group.

Wright

I guess the new buzz word "multitasking" is old hat to a pilot, then.

Maciolek

It really is. It prepared me very well for becoming a commander.

Wright

Greg, with this book, *Mission Possible!,* we're trying to encourage people in our audience and our readers to live better and to be more fulfilled by listening to the examples of our guests. Is there anyone in your life who has helped you to become a better person?

Maciolek

I know this is going to sound corny, but it is my parents. My dad's going to be ninety-nine this year, and my mom eighty-six. My dad has experienced some dementia in the last two or three years, so he really doesn't know who we are anymore. But let me tell you the influence my parents had on me. This is why I think parenting is so key. My parents raised six of us. My parents were both factory workers, but we always went on a vacation every year. We may not have had the latest things, but we always had everything we needed. We wore hand-me-downs.

There were two things my dad taught me. He told me, "Greg, learn how to type." He made all his kids take typing. Because I learned how to type, I was able to earn my way through college. I worked full time as a production clerk at Chevrolet while I went to school full time so I could get my degree. We didn't have scholarships and all these grants you have today. If I wanted to go to college, I needed to earn my way through it. Four out of the six of us earned our college degrees.

The other thing he said was, "Always go to work every day, because your boss depends on you." He said, "When you're at work, learn other people's jobs so you're more valuable to the boss." I'll tell you, that has never failed me. I go to work every day. Rarely do I ever miss work. They used to have to send me home because I always felt it was my obligation to go.

When I look at my parents' attitude toward people, there are a couple of things that come to mind. One is that no one is any better than anybody else. That has always served me well. I have always been able to relate with anyone regardless of his or her status. I met General Colin Powell when he was the Chairman of the Joint Chiefs of Staff. He treated me just like anybody else, and we had a very comfortable visit. I asked him to spend some time talking with the maintenance troops. He spent over thirty minutes with them, posing for pictures and everything. He even brought over the visiting Russian generals to pose for pictures as well. I've met some pretty high-level people, and I've also worked on a production line and as a truck loader. I've never had a problem relating to people.

I think another great philosophy my parents taught me was to always care about other people. The best example I have was when my mother's sister and her husband died. They had five kids under the age of fourteen. My parents were raising six kids of their own, but through their generosity, and with the help of my cousins' grandparent, they kept my cousins together. Four out of the five of them received degrees—engineering, school teaching, fine arts degrees. I learned that giving to others will always come back to you in the long run. I think God has rewarded them with a long and a happy life.

They will celebrate sixty-six years of marriage this year. They had a profound effect on my brothers and sisters and me and many others. I think most parents understand the impact they have long term on their kids and why it's so important to be there for them, especially in their formative years. It is the same for leaders of any organization as well. The leadership, decision making and example impacts their company and workers.

Wright

What a great conversation! I really appreciate your taking the time to be with me here on *Mission Possible!* today. It's been very enlightening and interesting, and I want to thank you so much. We have been talking today with Gregory J. Maciolek. His company approaches organizational health and integrity as a holistic endeavor. Greg, thank you so much for being with us.

Maciolek

David, it was a pleasure.

Gregory J. Maciolek, President
Integrated Management Resources, Inc.
PO Box 31933
Knoxville, Tennessee 37930-1933
Toll Free: 800.262.6403
Office: 865.539.3700
Fax: 865.531.8897
Email: greg.maciolek@imrtn.com
www.integratedmanagementresources.com

Chapter 8

MAUREEN G. MULVANEY, CSP

Maureen G. Mulvaney, better known as MGM, is an internationally known speaker who has graced the stages from Finland to Malaysia....spoken with everyone from Norman Vincent Peale to Ann Jillian...&....is a Certified Speaking Professional. (Only a handful of the 3000 plus members of National Speakers Association have ever been able to attain this earned designation because one must have both longevity in the speaking industry plus outstanding speaking skills....MGM has both!) MGM is also the author and co-author of: The Stress Strategist, Any Kid Can Be a Super Star, Chicken Soup for the Teacher's Soul and Stinky David. Maureen Welcome to Mission Possible.

The Interview

David E. Wright (Wright)

Today we're talking with Maureen G. Mulvaney, better known as MGM. Maureen is an internationally known speaker, who has graced stages from Finland to Malaysia. She has spoken on the platform with everyone from Dr. Norman Vincent Peale to Ann Jillian, and she is a Certified Speaking Professional (CSP). There's only a handful out of the 4,000-plus members of the National Speakers Association that have ever been able to attain this earned designation, because one must have both longevity in the speaking industry and outstanding speaking skills. Maureen has both. She is also the author and co-author of *Stress Strategist, Any Kid Can Be a Superstar, Chicken Soup for the Teacher's Soul* and *Stinky David*. Maureen, welcome to *Mission Possible!*

Maureen G. Mulvaney (Mulvaney)

Thank you, David. It's great to be here.

Wright

Let me ask you: Who tagged you with MGM as a nickname?

Mulvaney

That was my mama. She is very, very Irish, and she wanted the name to be Maureen G. Mulvaney, better known as MGM, her big production. She did that because she was the queen of positive space repetition. She used to send me, through the mail, things that said, "I always knew my MGM would be a big production one day" from the time I was in kindergarten. The number one fear in the nation is speaking; number seven is death, which means that more people would rather die than get up and speak. I grew up to be a speaker, and I think it was simply because my mother named me MGM, her big production.

Wright

It's hard to have a low self-image when you're called someone's major production.

Mulvaney

There you go!

Wright

You call yourself a "superstar attitude technologist." What is an attitude technologist?

Mulvaney

It's a term I coined, attitude technologist. It's because I work with people who want to drive themselves and their organizations to be number one, and they want a systematic road map to get them there. In my presentations and my book, I provide a systematic road map or guide, if you will, of strategies and techniques to drive participants to their greatest potential and success. They usually learn to define and support attitudes that are positive, create personal skills that are productive and then develop behaviors that can sustain long-lasting change. I believe greater productivity translates into greater financial rewards and happiness. It's my passion; it's my absolute passion to develop people in ways so that they become superstars in their own profession and in their lives.

Wright

You think attitude is more applicable than skills when hiring someone?

Mulvaney

In today's marketplace, you bet I do. I believe that in the past, we hired people because they were technically good at what they wanted to do. And now, David, I don't care about their technical skills. I want a positive attitude, because we hire people because of their technical skills, but we fire people because of their lack of personal skills or their lack of a positive attitude or an attitude that's going to be productive. Therefore, I believe positive attitudes lead to positive productive behaviors and skills. You can have the greatest skills in the world, but if you're hard to get along with and you gossip all the time and you don't get your work done on time, you don't make your commitments. Sure, I believe that is non-productive in today's marketplace.

Wright

Maureen, with our *Mission Possible!* talk show and book we're trying to encourage people in our audience and our readers to live better and be more fulfilled by listening to the examples of our guests. What has been the greatest comeback that you have made from adversity in your career or in your life?

Mulvaney

I'm a Baby Boomer, David, and like most Baby Boomers, we've been on a quest our whole lives to find success and the whole attitude surrounding success. I have played football, I've walked on fire, I've even sky dived to push past my own fears so that I could survive and thrive in the business world to attain financial and career success. So in the '90s my business was thriving, and I thought, "What other attitudes and success could I possibly need?" Well, there were new books and studies that were coming out all the time that showed we have to be reinvented for the future, for the year 2000 and beyond. These were telling us that we needed to encourage self-management skills, learn risk taking, cooperation, negotiation, personal control and growth. In the past, these were things that would just be nice, but nowadays they were telling us that they were going to be mandatory. They told us that top-down football-style management was going to be out and that less rigid spider web management was going to be in. The best place to be in a spider web would be in the middle and then to work your way out, to reach out instead of reaching down. Intuition, creativity, innovation were going to be mandatory for the year 2000 and beyond, as would excellent communication and people that could settle disputes calmly and cheer others on. Strength and endurance—all of these things were things we were going to need.

And I thought, "How was I ever going to learn how to do all these?" Then it dawned on me—motherhood. Really, is there a mom out there that doesn't have to cheer a family on to daily success? Is there a mother out there who doesn't know how to feed, change and diaper a baby while cleaning, washing and writing business reports? Is there a mom that doesn't know how to calmly settle a dispute? My mom should have been sent to settle with Saddam Hussein. By the time she was finished with him, he'd be apologizing for his bad behavior. Motherhood would surely teach me those business successes for the future, and it would really make a lifelong dream come true.

So, I decided I wanted to have a child. Well, I'd gone through a marriage and it had been childless, and when I divorced, I thought that yearning for having a child would go away, but it never did. One day a friend said, "Why don't you just adopt, Maureen. MGM, go get a baby." I said, "Well gosh, I think that's a great idea." For five years, David, I tried to adopt in the United States, and it just didn't look like it was going to happen. Then I heard about this doctor in Cambodia who was helping divorced single parents like me adopt orphaned Cambodian children. It was the perfect solution. I could save a child from a life of poverty and then make a lifelong dream come true to become a mom.

The challenges in the paperwork were astronomical, and I had to develop these tremendous self-management skills to deal with them. It finally became painfully clear that all the money, energy and paperwork would be in vain unless I could fly to Cambodia. Having learned to be flexible, I made the arrangements, and I was so flexible that I flew to a country that had no diplomatic relationship with the United States at that time, and it was in the middle of a raging civil war. But like a dope, I got on that plane and made the trek. As I arrived in the well-known vacation spot of Cambodia, I was so excited. You wouldn't have believed it. There I was. Talk about the ugly American with the video camera shooting the scenery. All of a sudden, a soldier came up to me, grabbed the camera, pushed me back against the plane, and was speaking a language I didn't understand. Finally, I negotiated with him and said, "Please, sir, I'll keep my camera if you'll take this money I want to give you." I found out real quickly that Cambodia was not a vacation spot and gift money works well in Cambodia.

When I got to the orphanage, the doctor and the agency had selected a little six-month-old baby, but when I walked through the door of that orphanage, I fell in love and gave birth through my heart to the most gorgeous one-week-old baby girl. Oh my gosh! Like magic, this little girl became soul of my soul and light of my life. Before I had time to revel in the excitement, the next challenge presented itself. If I changed babies, it would take at least a year to get the new paperwork. So using all my creativity and communication skills, I asked the orphanage director to switch the babies' paperwork instead. I thought that was very flexible; focus on the positive, get to the goal. To my surprise, the director said she'd do it! Of course, David, that gift money did not hurt!

Joyously, I became a mama, and I named my angel Makayla—Mikki for short—G. Mulvaney; MGM, my big production. For a week, we stayed in Cambodia to complete all the necessary paperwork and to give out all the gift money, of course, but I just focused on my little MGM. I was filled with ecstasy, and my MGM was just such a gift. Upon leaving Cambodia, the ecstasy was quickly shattered when our paperwork was missing one signature, so we couldn't get out of the country. To make matters worse, that same day I received a fax from my mom saying that my dad, who was in the final stages of his battle with cancer, had taken a turn for the worse and the family needed me to come home. So a heartbreaking decision had to be made—stay or go. Calmly, I focused on the positive and I persuaded these two American doctors who hated paperwork to bring my baby out if I took care of their babies' immigration paperwork. They agreed. Then immediately, I flew back to the United States to be with my dad and wait for baby MGM to come. It seemed like an eternity, but still focusing on the positive, my baby and I were reunited about two weeks later in the United States. Immediately, I grabbed little Mikki up and traveled from my home in Arizona to my parents' home in Maryland, and my family was overjoyed.

Little Mikki was the sunshine, joy, and laughter we needed as we watched my father deteriorate in the advanced stages of cancer. Mikki was showered with love by everybody, especially my dad. Oh, David, he idolized this new little angel grandchild. He would hold her for hours; it was like pain medicine to him. Week after week, month after month, our standard routine was travel to Maryland to visit my dad. To keep up our spirits, my mom, who is so funny, boobytrapped the whole house. She had these musical toilet paper holders called "Toity Tunes" in every one of the bathrooms. *The Star Spangled Banner* played in the main bathroom, and guests didn't know whether to stand and salute or wipe; they just didn't know! Then there were always colorful balloons filled with hot air floating around and plenty of relatives and friends floating around with hot air, too. We had few opportunities to laugh until baby Mikki was there, because we had only cried buckets of tears for my dad. We were sent this little angel in the form of my Mikki, and we just loved her.

I don't know how to tell you this next part, David, other than just to tell you what happened. Four months after Mikki had arrived, we had to go home to Arizona to have her checked out medically, and we were going right back to see my dad when the most unthinkable thing happened. It's a parent's worst nightmare. My special angel of joy, Mikki, died in her sleep. Wave after wave of shock was sent through my body as I picked up my lifeless little baby who, just hours before, had been smiling and full of life. And now she was gone. My whole life was gone, too. The police and the fire department and the neighbors stormed into the house, and they grabbed little MGM away from me. At first they said it was SIDS, and later they discovered it was a rare blood disease. But it didn't matter, because Mikki was gone.

I screeched like a wounded animal, and even now, I have tears rolling down my face. I apologize for that, but this was so devastating. Before I could even feel the intensity of what had happened, the automatic protective covering of my body, numbness, kicked in, and I sat in a daze. I stopped functioning on a conscious level at that time. My heart was beating, my lungs breathed and my blood flowed, but my life was gone, because my heart, which had given birth to this glorious child, was broken. I didn't think I would ever, ever love again like I had loved this Mikki, and the pain of the loss was absolutely astronomical. This numbness had almost totally encased me and mummified me when the next shock wave happened. My father, when he heard his beloved little Mikki had died, also let go of life and died eight hours later. Once again, I just screamed; I just screeched. I don't even know how to describe layers and layers and layers of pain with me sandwiched somewhere in between. There just aren't any words. My heart was simply broken for good.

Eventually, I can tell you that that protective numbness subsided, and I'd love to tell you how brave I was, but my first response was total, overwhelming despair. I dropped to my knees and I pleaded with God, "Please take me because I really don't want to go on living.

Mission Possible!

My heart is so heavy, and my arms are so very empty. Just let me come to you, because I just can't go on like this." I believe God heard me. I believe He listened to my plea for death, and I believe He understood, but the answer He gave me was a resounding, "No, I have a different plan for you." If my maker was going to let me live, surely I would find out the secret, the trick or the easy way to remove this pain and hurt and get through this horrible tragedy.

So day and night I prayed, "What is the secret, God? Just tell me. How do I get through this?" And finally, my prayers were answered. It's interesting, but I unwillingly had been lovingly and mercifully prepared to handle this horrible twist of fate, because I knew the secret; I just couldn't see it at that particular time. You see, in the 1970s I had played powder puff football to learn the great career secret. I had read Og Mandino's book *The Greatest Salesman in the World*, and it had taught me to learn from the wisdom of others. I kept waiting for that coach to tell me the secret, the trick, the easy way, how to get through playing football. The lesson I learned was to toughen up and get to the goal. The secret was that the choice was mine. Clearly, David, that coach wasn't talking about toughening up to hit and tackle the other team or your job or your material wealth. He was talking about tackling your life. I had to toughen up to hit back against the terrible hurt and the pain that just rocked my soul. I had to tackle the tough assignments of going to double wakes, double funerals and double memorial services. Football had taught me to toughen up and get to the goal, to do the things we have to do, regardless of the lack of desire to do them. The secret was so clear. I could whine, or I could choose to tackle my life and just go on, to learn Og Mandino's principle of persisting until I succeeded.

I had even once fire walked, and fire walking had taught me how to get to great material success by getting rid of my addiction to comfort. I kept waiting for the instructor to give me the secret or trick or easy way to that. The lesson of that instructor was burned in my head, because he kept saying, "For every negative thought, there is a positive thought; focus on the positive. Fire can either cause you great pain or it can heal you, and the choice is yours. Choose healing and walk across that fire." And I got it. He wasn't talking about the hot coals on the beach that night. He was talking about the fires of your life. We've all had fires in our lives. It doesn't have to be the loss of a loved one. It can be any hurt or any pain that you've had to go through or endure. The most comfortable choice would be fear; we know it. Fear would give us the perfect excuse to lie down, physically and mentally, and say, "I don't want to go on." How tempting that was for me. But the secret was so clear: I could continue to be immobilized by the comfort of fear, or I could choose to face my own pain, walk through that fire and just go on to relief.

At another time, I had also skydived so I could learn Og Mandino's success principle of seeking guidance. I took skydiving lessons, because I thought there was no better way to seek guidance than to jump out of a plane without a parachute! The one that had the parachute was the instructor. The lessons of that instructor floated back to me as he kept saying, "Let go. Stop resisting and go with the flow." Skydiving wasn't a daredevil stunt done by a crazy, wild woman; it was my leap of faith. I had to place the total trust in my abilities in someone else's hands—literally in their hands. It dawned on me that for me to heal, I was going to have to take huge leaps of faith. I'd always, always been considered the strong one. I was there for everyone, and I handled everything until it just got too painful, and I had to take a leap of faith and let go of this strong-woman image. I had to take a leap of faith and stop resisting the help from other people. I had to trust my friends to guide me through the physical tasks and trust my family to tenderly protect my fragile ego and emotions. Finally, I had to take a leap of faith so I could let go and place my life in the capable hands of my Lord. And so the secret became very, very clear. I could choose to go on and stay in hurt and pain, or I could choose to take leaps of faith by letting go of the past, accepting my blessings in the present and just go on.

Lastly, I begged God for the trick, the easy way to take the pain away. This was the wildest thing that happened. My answer came in the most unusual way. After the funeral, when all the friends and relatives had gone home and I was there all by myself, the days that followed were very dark and sometimes so tough to get through. Some days I got through them and some days I didn't. One day, I was sitting there, just sobbing. The grief and sadness and loneliness had overwhelmed me like a tidal wave. I was crying uncontrollably when all of a sudden, I just felt a presence. As I wiped my eyes and looked up there before me, I saw my dad and baby Mikki in the form of angels. They were surrounded with a brilliant white halo, and my father was holding baby Mikki. They came walking toward me, and my father said, "MGM, I heard your plea to give in and come with us, but darling, it's not your time. It was my time, and I was sent to take care of our dear little Mikki, and we're happy. I want you to know we're at peace."

He said, "Now let's talk about you. You've always been so filled with love and light and joy, but since our departure, you've let all the pain fill you up, and your light's been turned off. It's time for you to open your heart and let the love and joy back in so you fly with the angels." Well David, I'm Irish, and we Irish love a good fight. I just looked at my dad and said, "Are you crazy? Dad, open my heart again after it's been crushed in a million pieces? How can I ever choose to let go and let the love in again?" My father quietly said, "Maureen, you've spent a lifetime seeking success through gaining wealth and power and things. You thought mega success would make you happy, but it was the love of Mikki that truly made you happy. It's time to let go of that pain. It's time to open your heart again and let that love and joy that surrounded you come back in so you can fly with the angels. The choice is yours."

And then my father smiled, and little Mikki smiled, and then they waved and walked back into the light. I just went, "Wow," and at that moment I became a believer. David, I can't explain to you how I could walk on 1,500 degrees of fire and not get burnt. Neither can the scientists. They don't know how that happens, but people do it all the time. Likewise, I can't explain how I saw two angels, but I did, and from that moment on, all the pain, all the grief, all the sadness that had so overwhelmed me just went "whoosh." It was gone. My father had really helped me to understand that I had to get up and go on. I had things to do.

In November 1992, I traveled around the world again, and this time, my adoption journey took me to Viet Nam. I fell in love and gave birth through my heart to a one-and-a-half-year-old baby girl, a living angel. I named her Mayre G. Mulvaney, MGM, my big production. The orphanage considered Mayre unadoptable because she had a gaping cleft palate, respiratory disease and hearing loss, but I just called her my dream come true, my earth angel, my little miss wings. To tell you the truth, today Mayre is twelve years old. She is learning the attitudes and principles of having a successful life by learning the Og Mandino Success System that helped me through so much of my pain. She is confident and she's self-assured, because she knows she's nature's greatest miracle and that she's my little superstar.

Wright

What a story! If you could have a platform and tell our audience and our readers something that you feel would help or encourage them, what would you say?

Mulvaney

I'd have to say that you have to make the choice. Things happen in life, they really do, and you have to make that choice to live fully and joyously. Everyone has hard knocks, but I wanted to give Mayre a system, a way she could get through life so when the hard times came, she'd know what to do. And it was with Og Mandino. When Og Mandino helped me through so much of my stuff, I began reading him again. I discovered his book, *The Greatest Salesman in the World,* but he also came out with a system called *The Og Mandino Success System for the 21st Century*. Mayre and I have gone through this system so that we could both become our greatest, and it is life-changing. Mayre and I went through the system together, and the assessment was unbelievable. It gives you a crystal clear picture of where you are right now, and it doesn't compare you with others; it just compares you with yourself to show you your self-starting ability, your self-esteem, your balanced decision making, all those kinds of things. So it showed Mayre her strengths. It showed her what her potential was. It was a diagnosis, if you will, of where she is right now. Then, armed with that information, we both went through the training and the workbook and classroom experience, all of which were incredible. It's a guide to living life well. For a child, she has learned these lessons because it's exciting, it's different, it's interesting, and they give you the principles to live by. Make and keep commitments. Greet each day with love in your heart. Persist until you succeed. Know that you have value and are appreciated whether anyone else in the world appreciates you or not.

So, Mayre is using these principles to navigate her way through middle school, which is no easy task. It has given me the principles to navigate through the business world and to absolutely improve my business so that I can survive and thrive. If I were to say one thing, that would be it. We Irish believe that crying cleanses the soul of sadness, but laughing revives the soul. One of the skills in the system is laughing at the world. Sometimes you're thrown curves, and sometimes extraordinary things happen to very ordinary people. It's not what happens to you in life, but what choices you make about life. So make the choice to live life to its fullest and, like Og Mandino says, become the greatest you.

Wright

Let me ask you one final question. Is there anything or anyone in your life that has made a difference for you and helped you become a better person?

Mulvaney

I'd have to say, of course, my greatest heroes in my life have obviously been my mom and dad. My mother opened the way; she was the queen of space repetition. She led me to these principles. She was always, always thinking to give us ways that we'd have not only our background and our belief in God but other ways that we could have things to hold onto. When she introduced me to Og Mandino, his writings, his books and his beliefs, they really were life changing. I think for me, my Mayre and for the people that I work with in my seminars, it is truly an experience to give you power in your life, to bring success into your life and give you principles that are the only things that endure. You can gain and lose complete wealth, but principles endure. Children today are desperately seeking something, but they don't know where to look. I think these are the two things that helped me—my parents' ability to teach me and to open up the world to me and Og Mandino giving me a systematic guide to get me to where I want to be in my life. Bringing joy, happiness and kindness to other people and reaching out to touch other peoples' hearts and souls—that's what I try to do.

Wright

What a wonderful conversation! You are a delight. You are really a role model for all of us.

Mulvaney

I so appreciate that.

Wright

What a great story. We have been talking this morning with Maureen G. Mulvaney. She's better known as MGM. A great, great presentation. She is an internationally known speaker. She is an author and, as we have learned today, she is a lady who has things in order, has her priorities straight and believes in living to the fullest. Thank you so much for being with us, Maureen.

Mulvaney

Thank you, and if your guests wish to reach me, they can get to me at www.mgmsuperstar.com. We'd love to have them visit and chat with them at any time.

Maureen G. Mulvaney, CSP
MGM & Associates, Inc.
16026 S. 36th Street
Phoenix, Arizona 85048-7322
Toll Free: 800.485.0065
Fax: 480.759.6257
Email: mgm@mgmsuperstar.com
www.mgmsuperstar.com

Chapter 9

CHRISTINE HOLTON CASHEN

Christine combines a down-to-earth attitude with a colorful artistic streak. Drawing from her experience in university admissions, training, broadcasting and theatre, this award-winning speaker has presented throughout the United States, Canada, South Africa and Australia. Christine holds a Bachelors Degree in Communication and a Masters Degree in Adult Education. She is a professional member of the National Speakers Association who delivers interactive humor, conflict and creativity programs that are chock full of fun and useful tools.

The Interview

David E. Wright (Wright)

Today we're talking with Christine Holton Cashen. Christine is an award-winning and highly recognized speaker who has presented during the past eight years to thousands of individuals throughout the United States, Canada, South Africa and Australia. Christine holds her bachelor's degree in communication and master's degree in adult education. What makes her unique is her ability to be real. Drawing from her varied background as a business owner, university admissions officer, corporate trainer and broadcaster, she combines a

Mission Possible!

down-to-earth attitude with a colorful artistic streak. She is a professional member of the National Speaker's Association and an authority on sparking, innovative ideas to handle conflict, reduce stress and energize employees. Christine is featured regularly as a creative expert in *HOW Designs at Work* magazine. Christine, welcome to *Mission Possible!*

Cashen

Thanks, David.

Wright

In your program entitled Get What You Want with What You've Got, you state that communicating effectively is a function of understanding personality styles. What do you mean?

Cashen

Oftentimes, we speak in our own language rather than the language of the person we are speaking with. In order to communicate effectively, we need to learn to shift to the other person's style and focus on his or her concerns. For example, if you are speaking with someone who is very focused, you need to make sure that you get to the point very quickly, rather than beating around the bush. If, on the other hand, you are talking to someone who thrives on social interaction, you need to take the time for the social pleasantries. If you are too focused, the social person will challenge you, sometimes sarcastically. He or she will say, "Aren't you going to say, 'Good morning? How's your family? How was your weekend?'" You need to take the time for the pleasantries, even though it might not be your style, in order to communicate with this person more effectively.

I have to shift my focus all the time. My husband is more analytical than I am. It is not my style to provide all of the details and to actually think through what I'm saying before I say it. In conversations with him, however, I really need to do both. Otherwise, we have moments when I say to him, "Guess what! I'm speaking in San Antonio. Let's go for the weekend," and I expect him to simply say, "Yes." He, however, comes back with a list of questions: "Well, how much are the tickets? How long are we going to be there? Are there any golf courses in the area? How much free time will you have?" Of course, I haven't thought through any of these details. I'm only thinking, "It's an adventure. Let's go!" He will step out of his comfort zone and agree to my adventure, but only when I have provided the details. Details make my eyes glaze over, and spontaneity makes his stomach turn. We communicate more effectively, though, when we recognize each other's focus.

Wright

Through the years I've had a lot of training and interest in personality-style testing such as the DISC or the Myers-Briggs. Is that what you're talking about?

Cashen

It's great to take those tests. I think, however, that we are all tested out. I've known people that dread "one more personality test." I think we need to spend less time labeling our own personality style and more time learning to match the communication style and focus of the people we are living and working with, in order to relate to these people more effectively.

Wright

So you treat them the way they want to be treated.

Cashen

Exactly.

Wright

In the same program, you talk about diffusing anger and handling conflict. Could you give our audience and readers some tips on how to do this?

Cashen

Now more than ever, we need to become aware of how we handle conflict. I think the problem with the way we deal with anger and conflict is that we always focus on the other person or people in the situation. We say, "That person made me mad," or "I can't believe that person said that or did that." We need to recognize, however, that our own reactions to each situation create the outcome.

Then we need to take charge of our reactions. I will be honest with you; I've been struggling with this for a long time. I'm Irish-Italian and grew up with a lot of overt conflict. In my family, you yell, scream, rant and rave, and then you move on. I thought everyone did this, that it was normal behavior. Then I learned that some families don't talk at all about the conflict they feel or experience. For example, my sister-in-law doesn't get mad at her husband; she just shrinks his golf shirts. She grew up in a different type of family. Our tendency is to handle conflict as we were raised to handle it. But we all need to recognize that we are thermostats, not thermometers. A thermometer only reacts; thermostats can be controlled. Of course, we are going to react at times, but we're more in control of our behaviors than we realize. It can be powerful to simply stop, take a deep breath and say, "Hold up. I'm not going to let this rude driver ruin my day." Rude drivers usually don't know how rude they are, because they're focused on going about their business. Even though they are oblivious, we can spend three hours after the event reliving the moment we were cut off and thinking about what we should have done. We just don't realize how much we let other people affect us personally.

Wright

So rather than trying to change other people or diffuse their anger, you're saying that it's up to you to handle your own anger management.

Cashen

Exactly. We need to take control of ourselves and stop saying everything happens "because of other people."

Wright

So you have no responsibility for another person's actions, only the way you react to him or her.

Cashen

David, it is a waste of time to try to change other people—other drivers, other people in line, co-workers, clients. You just can't. People behave the way they do because they're getting something out of it. Their behavior works for them.

Wright

Right.

Cashen

People who are rude and aggressive obviously have been getting the service they want by being rude and aggressive. They are not going to change simply because you tell them they are behaving badly. You have to think, instead, about what you can do to deal with that type of behavior.

Wright

Was it Abraham Lincoln who said that people are about as happy as they make up their minds to be?

Cashen

Yes.

Wright

Christine, you've been called a fun expert, and you advocate humor for reducing stress, increasing job satisfaction, improving health and creating higher productivity. Is humor really that important?

Cashen

Now more than ever. I think we as individuals and as a country need the healing power of laughter and humor to deal with tragedies, stress, the economy, jobs and downsizing. Humor keeps you flexible. If you don't have humor, you're going to break.

Wright

A few years ago, my wife went through a terrible bout with cancer. I think everybody thought she was going to die. She and I were in several support groups, those groups that they put people in after surgery and chemotherapy. Through the groups, we were introduced to books on humor. I believe humor really does work.

Cashen

Studies have proven that laughter works. It has the power to heal, reduce stress levels and release hormones; it's a great cardiovascular workout, you know. Have you ever laughed so hard that you couldn't stand up? Laughter is a muscle relaxer with health benefits. Sometimes you don't even need anything to trigger the laughter; you can deliberately start to laugh and create the same endorphin flow in your body. Endorphins are God's drugs as far as I'm concerned.

Wright

You also talk about twenty practical tips for reducing stress that can be put into action immediately. Could you give us just a few?

Cashen

Rather than focus only on traditional stress techniques such as deep breathing, I like to teach people unique things that they can do at work and at home. One of them is to identify the relatively insignificant events that trigger their anger. I call these our societal pet peeves—you know, those commonsense things that we think people should know, but don't. For example, it is inappropriate to clip your nails in public, snap your gum or put toilet paper any way but over the top of the roll. The reality is, however, that we all have different commonsense rules, and this variety creates a lot of unnecessary stress.

I try to encourage people to save their stress for the big stuff and not to obsess over these little rules that are broken. Sometimes, before you get to the office, you may see twenty of your rules broken. If you do not shift perspective, you will be completely upset and frustrated by the time you pull into the parking lot. Before you even start your workday, you will be angry simply because one person didn't use his or her turn signal, another person wouldn't get out of the left lane on the highway and someone else is in "your" parking space, even though your name is not on that space.

We have to remember that we have a choice to let these events affect us or not. I know some people who let go of their pet peeves and others who are peeved continually through the day. To those of you who are continually peeved, I encourage you to make up a story about the rule breaker's past. Let's be clear: You don't tell the offender this story; it's just for you. In other words, if people don't use their turn signals, instead of getting mad, you think to yourself, "Aw, those people didn't have enough money to get that option on their cars." Maybe they're out of turn signal fluid, or maybe their left arms are broken, preventing them from safely triggering that mechanism. Maybe the people who drive by you like maniacs are going to the hospital because they're having a baby. Or maybe they are trying not to miss their flight. Some of your difficult clients might not be taking their medication regularly, making them a little cranky or irrational. You just don't know what triggers behavior. By making up a story, you have more compassion for the people.

Sometimes your story might even be correct. I had an evil boss once whom I used to dislike very much until I came to the conclusion that she had never known love. Hurt people want to hurt people. Loving people want to love people. Thanks to that realization about my boss, when I encounter someone who is unkind or rude, I understand that this person must be damaged on the inside to want to damage someone on the outside.

Wright

You have taken your thoughts into your own hands, and you have been proactive.

Cashen

Exactly. Plus, it's fun to make up the stories. Sometimes when you lose perspective, you don't realize what you're saying in front of your children or other people, especially in the car. When you get angry, you cause anxiety and stress for your passengers. It is better to make up a story, reduce the stress and create a little bit of humor.

Mission Possible!

Wright

Christine, you have just solved the complex question about signaling in the state of Tennessee. From now on, when I look at a car with a Tennessee license plate and see the turn signal on, I will know that the signal is either broken or that it was like that when the driver bought the car.

Cashen

I love that.

Wright

We don't use signals much in Tennessee.

Cashen

Because it's nobody's business where you're going, right?

Wright

Well put. Most of us have heard that we need to build relationships with our clients. It sounds good, but many of us don't know where to start. Can you give us some advice?

Cashen

We just need to be real people. I can't tell you how many times I've talked to people on the phone who sound as if they're reading a script. As the caller, you're not treated like a person at all. Recently, I called a car rental agency. As the young man was totaling my rate, he said, "Congratulations. You have earned a free gas voucher worth twenty dollars." For fun, I went crazy. I shouted excitedly, "You're kidding? Me? I won? I never win anything!" When I finished, he was totally silent on the other end of the phone. I had thrown him off his script completely, and he did not know how to handle it. Finally, I said, "Hello?" and in an unsure voice he replied, "Does that mean yes, you want it?" Had he set aside his script, laughed and said, "Yes, you did! You are the lucky caller," I would have laughed and accepted the voucher for just about anything. Instead, I did not rent from this company at all, because he was not real. Although it is important to be efficient and stick to business, sometimes that extra comment or connection with somebody can really make a difference. This connection can be made easily. For example, I could ask you where you are from. Just knowing that piece of information, I could mention a friend of mine in Tennessee and the connection would be made.

Wright

So you try to find common denominators?

Cashen

Exactly.

Wright

You know, I've been booking speakers now for about thirteen years. I've probably read more books, watched more videos and heard more cassette tapes on the subject of customer service than many other topics. Yet customer service seems to be at an all-time low. Why do you think that is?

Cashen

Wow. I don't know if there's a general sense of apathy or if people just aren't working at jobs they feel passionate about. People have to put passion in what they do, whatever it is. I think so many people are settling for careers they don't enjoy and then counting down the days until they can retire. Some people retire and just don't tell anybody. They should tell everyone, if only to get a party.

Wright

Right. You know, even when I go into a fast food restaurant, I want them to be nice to me first and then hurry if they can. Simply being nice is really important in customer service.

Cashen

Yes, it is sad that we get so excited when we get good service. When someone actually treats you well and gives you a smile, you feel as though you have won the lottery. That should be the norm rather than the exception. I think the bottom line is this: People who work in customer service should visualize every customer wearing a sign that says, "Make me feel important and make me look good." Too often, customers feel like interruptions in the worker's day because the worker doesn't make people feel very important.

Wright

Creativity is lacking in many companies, and new ideas seem to be at a premium. How do we unleash our creativity to help our companies and help ourselves succeed?

Cashen

When I am brought in by companies to speak on creativity, one of the biggest problems I see is the premature death of new ideas. Oftentimes, companies use the word "brainstorming" to describe what is actually a brain drizzle or a brain drought. In these droughts, employees get together, sit around a circular table with some doughnuts in the middle, and someone says, "Go." Then every idea is shot down by criticism. Members of the group will say, "Oh no, we tried that before," "We don't have the money," "We don't have the staff" and "Oh, you must be new here." We need to replace these droughts and drizzles with real brainstorming. Let's take it to new heights and create brain El Nino. Responses to ideas should be comments like, "Good for you," "I'm so glad you're thinking about this" and "What a neat idea. Let's take a look at that."

Now in an effort to be supportive, some people say there's no such thing as a stupid idea. That's a lie. There are a lot of stupid ideas. But sometimes you can piggyback on a stupid idea to make it a great idea. In order to do so, however, you have to give all ideas a chance. I teach groups to set ground rules that foster creative problem solving. No killer phrases are allowed. No ideas are judged in the beginning. You can, of course, judge ideas to death later in the process but not in the beginning.

In the beginning, come up with ideas by playing the "what if" game. In this game, you are required to come up with twenty-five solutions to a given problem. You can only come up with all twenty-five by really stretching, laughing and allowing humor into your meeting rooms. Sometimes the craziest ideas spawn the best ideas. Having an idea quota like the one detailed in the "what if" game is crucial to finding a couple of really good ideas. You're going to have some crazy ideas, but you're also going to have some good ones. Willingness to play, listen and suspend judgment opens up the lines of communication and creativity in a group.

Wright

As you were talking, I was thinking about what you said earlier about relationships. It is as if you apply the same philosophy to both creative problem solving and dealing with people. Prejudging might cause you to lose a brilliant idea or a lifelong relationship.

Cashen

Exactly. That's the way it was with my husband. Not until the third date did I realize what an am amazing guy he was. Prior to dating him, I usually had one date with a person and immediately thought, "Next." Giving people and ideas a chance yields great rewards.

Wright

With my wife, it was much easier. I just lied to her. I told her I was rich. It works most of the time.

Cashen

The original Joe Millionaire.

Wright

Christine, I've read that you come from a family of lunatics.

Cashen

True.

Wright

You've said you were shocked when you left home and found out how serious other people were. Have people lost their senses of humor, or did they simply just never have any?

Cashen

That is such a good question but a tough one. Deep down, I would like to believe that everyone has a sense of humor and that they simply haven't exercised it in a long time. Some people get terminal seriousness, hardening of the attitude, and they think things just aren't that funny anymore. This phenomenon breaks my heart, because having a sense of humor is such a sign of recovery in life. Think about it. When people leave the hospital and others ask family members about them, the family often says, "Well, we know they're okay because they have their sense of humor back. They were joking with the nurses." Humor is a sign of recovery. It scares me when people are so serious and have forgotten how to have fun. They are missing out on such an important and rewarding part of life.

Wright

I direct music for the Gatlinburg Community Chorale. A lady died last month that had been a member of the chorale for twenty-two years. Amazingly, I've never laughed as much in my life as I did at her funeral. All of the people who stood up told these funny stories about her. It was a celebration of the fun that she gave people all of her life. On the other hand, I have met people who have what you call "terminal seriousness." You know, these people make it really difficult to be around them.

Cashen

They really do. I just can't imagine living life with someone like that or being that person myself. I think that's very sad.

Wright

I have heard some trainers suggest simple things like putting cartoons up on the bulletin board in the coffee room—anything to make people laugh or lighten up a little. Do you agree with this?

Cashen

I say "Lighten up before you tighten up." I think everyone should have their own smile file, where you put things that crack you up. You can try nice cards from people or letters. A friend of mine sends herself postcards from everywhere she goes. She says no one cares about your vacations—not really. So, she sends postcards to herself back at the office instead of to others. She usually beats her postcards back to the office. She then receives them and they always say the same thing: "Wish you were here." She really means it. She says she can go on mini mental vacations anytime she wants by looking through those cards. Wow—that is the attitude. You know what's amazing, David? Instead of adopting this positive attitude, people sometimes compete to be the most stressed and miserable. Someone asks, "How are you doing?" and then the exchange continues like this: "I worked eighty hours last week." "I worked eighty-four." "Oh, yeah, well I didn't sleep at all last night." "Well, I haven't slept in the past year; you're pretty lucky." Whoever claims to be the most miserable actually thinks he's the winner.

Wright

It's like playing bridge or topping each other with their trumps.

Cashen

Exactly. Have you ever noticed that?

Wright

Yes, I have. You've been talking a lot about taking charge of your actions and being responsible for your own emotions. But how much do your emotions control your actions?

Cashen

Your thoughts actually create the emotions, and the emotions create the actions. First, I think, "I can't believe that guy made me mad. I can't believe what he did." These thoughts lead to emotions such as anger, pain and humiliation. The emotions cause the back of my neck to get hot and my face to get red. The emotion then leads to action. I might cry, storm out or say something I will regret. So you have to intervene at the level of the thought process. Say the word "stop," change your thoughts and get it together before those emotions come and create the actions.

Wright

Christine, your audiences have said that you are real, and they say that you seem to be talking directly to them. Do you share your struggles as well as your successes with them?

Cashen

You know, I don't think I share my struggles; I think I share our struggles. That makes the difference. I've been to many programs presented by people who have a big story to tell of their unique struggles. To be honest with you, I can't relate to them sometimes. When I speak about our shared struggles, I love to see audience members nodding their heads. I love when they come to me at the end of the program and say, "You have been in my house," "You have been in my office" or even, "I'm very scared right now, because you remind me of myself." Let me give you some examples. I talk about voice mail message pet peeves, specifically when people leave you a message and say their number so quickly that you have to listen to the message twenty times. And what about the people who mumble when they say their names? "Hi, David, this is garblegarblefafa." You call back and ask for Fafa, and the person who left you the message says, "Who?" You want to scream, "I don't know! You tell me!" In addition to the voice mail problems, we all have a phantom person in the office that jams the copy machine and then leaves. Everyone has had experiences like these. So when I speak, I see audience members laughing, nudging each other, nodding and even yelling out in agreement. I love to share the daily struggles that I've experienced that I know the majority of the audience has experienced too. Then we can come up with solutions together.

Wright

Christine, with this book we're trying to encourage people in our audience and our readers to live better and be more fulfilled by listening to the examples of our guests. Is there anything that you could add that might help our audience?

Cashen

My best advice is to become a life student. Many people think that once they're done with school, they're done with learning. Many of us are waiting for others to bring solutions to problems we have, when we can create the solutions on our own. We're our own CEOs, chief executive officers of ourselves. We need to ask ourselves what we are doing every day to increase our stock price. Are you working toward the life and relationships you want? Or are you playing the victim of circumstance? It doesn't take much to start moving toward the results you want. One or two changes that force you to step out of your normal routine will provide results. We are all busy. We are all stressed. We are all overwhelmed. Cry me a river! Ultimately, life is about priorities. It's about choices. It's about continual learning and implementation of what you learn.

Wright

There is so much going on for all of us. I honestly intend to read everything that comes across my desk, but there's so much, and I get so far behind. I feel as if I'm sitting in front of a fire hydrant drinking through a straw. The information just goes by me.

Cashen

There is so much out there, and you can't do everything at once. So you need to focus on one thing you want to work on. It might be communication, creativity or personality profiles. For me, right now, it's organization. When you go to a seminar or read a book, there are so many ideas that you don't always know where to start. To combat feeling overwhelmed, write down some of your favorite ideas, each one individually on an index card. Then put the cards in a bowl and pull out one every week or month that you're going to work on. Using this technique, the task seems manageable and you start taking one step at a time to make the changes that will lead to a very different life.

Wright

This is interesting. I'd like to ask you one final question. As I look back on my life, I can see people I appreciate who have made a profound difference or who have helped me to do things. Their good humor or something that they did for me changed me for the better. Do most of us have that in common? Are there any people in your life who have helped you to become a better person?

Cashen

There's no doubt. Anybody you ask can name two or three people, maybe more if they're fortunate. For some, it is family; for others, a coach, a person in high school or even a favorite babysitter. All of us know somebody who has had a big impact and influence on us. We need to take that influence and pass it on. Ask yourself, "Who can I help? Who could I positively influence?" Become a role model or mentor to somebody. I think that each of us is a palette. All of the people who influence us bring their own colors and brushstrokes that add to the paintings that are our lives.

Wright

That's a great analogy. I'll have to remember that.

Cashen

Of course, we are our own artists. We can paint over what someone has painted, or we can add to what someone has painted. Realize that a lot of people and influences color your picture, but you are ultimately in control of the brushstrokes.

Wright

This has been a great conversation. I really do appreciate your being with us today on *Mission Possible!* We've been talking today with Christine Holton Cashen. She is an award-winning and highly recognized speaker. She is also a professional member of the National Speaker's Association and is an authority on sparking innovative ideas to handle conflict, reduce stress and energize employees. You can learn more about her at www.adynamicspeaker.com. Christine, thank you so much for being with us today.

Cashen

Thank you, David.

Christine Holton Cashen
2802 Twin Coves Drive
Highland Village, TX 75077
Email: Christine@adynamicspeaker.com
www.adynamicspeaker.com

Chapter 10

TED GARRISON

Ted Garrison, president of Garrison Associates, combines over 25 years experience in the construction industry with numerous years of research to provide practical advice to his construction industry clients in the form of writings, including co-authoring four books and numerous article of industry publications; seminars and consulting services.

The Interview

David E. Wright (Wright)

Today we are talking with Ted Garrison. For over twenty-five years, Ted has worked in the construction and real estate industry. In addition to a civil engineering degree, he has practical experience working in framing crews, trim crews and survey crews. But most of his time has been spent in executive positions during the development and construction of almost a billion dollars worth of hotels, office buildings, office parks, storage facilities and public buildings. Recently, he was the director of construction on the Pennsylvania Convention Center, Pennsylvania's largest non-highway public works project in history. Therefore, he brings life experiences to the platform in his nearly 100 seminars and talks per year and also in his consulting work. Ted Garrison, welcome to *Mission Possible!*

Mission Possible!

Ted Garrison (Garrison)

Thank you.

Wright

Ted, there seems to be a greater emphasis today on leadership. Do you feel that way? If so, why is that?

Garrison

Yes, I agree. The answer is complex, because there are many contributing factors, but there are two issues that are especially critical. The first is that there is constant change in today's environment. It's both rapid and continuous. The world just keeps changing faster and faster and faster. In this type of environment, everyone needs to be able to function independently. There isn't time to wait for directions from above. Virtually everyone needs to be a leader and to be able to take charge and move forward to deal with the challenges they encounter on a daily basis. The U.S. Army has developed a new slogan, "An Army of One." A lot of baby boomers misunderstand the meaning of this slogan. They say it's ridiculous. Well, it's not. The slogan conveys the meaning that each solider has the necessary training to understand and carry out the mission. Obviously, if he is going against a large force, the soldier expects to be joined by other "armies of one," Each soldier has the attitude, "I'm properly trained, I know what to do, and I'm capable of carrying out the mission." In other words, even the private is not kept in the dark about the mission's goal.

The second issue is the increasing demands by customers. Customers want action now. They want it faster, cheaper and better. When senior management uses their lower level people to create a barrier between them and the customer, the customer's questions and problems get resolved too slowly. All employees must understand their role within the company and how to respond immediately to the customer's needs by following the company's vision instead of relying on specific directions from above.

Wright

So you are suggesting that we all, employees as well as management, should take on qualities of the leader?

Garrison

Absolutely. Leadership must start at the bottom of the organization. I recommend that companies start training their people on leadership on their employee's first day on the job. This is our military's concept today; they train everybody in leadership. The military used to believe that only certain people were capable of being leaders, while others were only capable of following orders. Changing this tradition has made our military a better fighting force. While leadership should be at every level of an organization, it's obvious that individuals at lower levels will have less responsibility. What is important is that all individuals are exercising leadership, and as they move up through the organization, they continue to develop their leadership skills. After all, leadership is a learned skill, and people must practice it as they grow and gain responsibility. In my seminars, I discuss a concept that I call a Strategic Goal©. I define it as "a project outcome that is mutually agreed upon and creates a win-win environment for all stakeholders." This means no matter what role an individual is playing, it's essential for that individual to understand everyone's needs in order to ensure an effective team. This requires leadership. For this to occur within an organization, its people must be out there dealing with the challenges and making decisions, whether the challenges involve customers, employees or people on either side of you, such as other contractors. We must work together, and that requires leadership. We need to avoid operating under a large set of rigid rules, which was the old way of doing things. People must be able to think for themselves and then adapt. This is the heart of leadership.

Wright

Could you give us a working definition of leadership?

Garrison

Everybody has his or her own definition. My favorite definition is General Eisenhower's. He defines leadership as, "the art of getting someone else to do something that you want done, because he wants to do it." When you stop and consider that Eisenhower was often get-

Mission Possible!

ting people to go get killed, the challenge for us to get people to do what we want should be a lot easier.

Wright

What, in your opinion, is the difference between leaders and managers?

Garrison

In my seminars on leadership, I have attendees take a little test. The test is to select one item from each of eight pairs of choices. The first choice is, "Do you administer, or do you innovate?" The second one is, "Do you copy, or do you originate?" Third, "Do you maintain, or do you develop?" Fourth, "Do you focus on systems and structures, or do you focus on the long-range perspective and people?" Number five, "Do you worry about how and when, or do you worry about what and why?" Number six, "Do you always worry about the bottom line, or do you look over the horizon?" Number seven, "Do you maintain the status quo, or do you challenge the status quo?" Number eight, and this is my favorite, "Do you do things right, or do you do the right things?" The reason the last one is my favorite is because it makes people think. They just aren't sure how to respond. It should be obvious that at different times we need both options. But the choice is about which way to lean.

The first part of each pair is what managers tend to do, while the second part of the pair is what leaders tend to do. When I ask people, "Should you do things right, or should you do the right thing," they think I'm crazy. But I follow up with another question: "What's the point of doing something extraordinarily well that doesn't need to be done?" This is why leadership is about doing the right things. It's better doing something at eighty percent that needs to be done than doing something at 100 percent that doesn't need to be done. Of course, the optimum solution is doing the right things and doing them right. That is a grand slam. Leadership is about getting people to focus on doing the right things and creating an environment that supports that idea. The reason many people often don't do the right thing is because they are scared of making a mistake. Often they lack experience in this area, so they are uncomfortable. They focus on things they are comfortable with, even if it's not important. We must learn to grade people on doing the right thing, not just on how well they do things.

Wright

It may very well be that with the problems that we've had in the recent past with the large corporations and issues of dishonesty and hiding certain things is that the people were really doing what they were told but that they didn't have the right information, and what they were doing was not right. Is that what you are trying to say?

Garrison

Integrity is a critical issue. The problem is that too many people worry about trying to maximize the company's profits or, in some cases, even worse, their own personal profits and not focusing on doing what's right. Recently, some people thought it was more important to portray their company as doing well instead of focusing on the truth that would allow the company to uncover any of its problems in order to correct them. This condition raises an important issue. First, those taking this approach were not very good leaders. But equally important, the lower-level people weren't showing leadership either by ignoring these conditions. When something isn't right, a leader speaks up, yet some of these companies attempt to dishonor those leaders who spoke up by calling them "whistle blowers." Of course, loyalty is an important aspect of leadership, but blindly supporting mistakes is not leadership but dereliction of duty. This doesn't mean that leadership is better than management or a replacement for it. We need managers. They do things like planning, budgeting, et cetera; therefore, we need both. However, we need a greater emphasis on leading people instead of controlling people, which is at the heart of leadership. Leadership is expanding instead of restricting. If you think about the above questions, you will understand it's about looking to the future and empowering people to do the job instead of telling everyone what to do.

Wright

What do you believe is the biggest problem concerning leadership?

Garrison

I'm not sure there is a single obstacle to leadership. Certainly, one is lack of existing leadership. I think too many senior people in companies have a manager's mentality. They feel like they must control everything and therefore have overly complex reporting procedures. They force people into boxes of their choice, because then they feel in control and believe it's safer. They think it's easier to tell people what to do than give them sufficient guidance to allow them to make their own decisions. Too many people overanalyze. Analysis is fine, but too often, companies are crippled by it. This is constant battle between the analytical left brain and the creative right brain. We need balance. Obviously, we have to analyze the facts, but if we box ourselves in by trying to make every decision based on pure numbers, we will have problems.

I think this is what has recently happened in business in general. For example, when there is an over-reliance on the company's stock performance, short-term decisions are made that are expedient versus doing the right thing. When you measure the CEO's performance based upon the stock price, then the managers will figure out how to manipulate or maximize the stock price instead of focusing on the long-term interest of the company. We have seen this happen in recent years, and when the bottom fell out, those companies were destroyed and went bankrupt. They included some of the largest companies in America. Leadership is about evaluating people on real performance, not just by some numbers. A lot of people have been coming out and criticizing how CEOs are hired based on performance of their stocks and given bonuses-based stock prices instead of what they are really doing to grow the company and make the company better. This is important, because doing the right things over time will produce a higher company value. Worrying about the stock price on a short-term basis, especially when companies often have no real control over the short-term value, leads to too many short-term decisions that are not right for the company.

It's easy to understand why people do this; they are merely responding to the rules that had been established. If you measure performance based solely upon the stock's performance, and if the person gets fired if the stock price drops, then you are going to have people focusing on the stock price instead of what's needed. Too often, we encourage people to be managers instead of leaders. Instead, we need leaders who understand this concept and sell the measure of real results. Everyone should be measured on real performance.

I believe another problem is that too many people find it difficult to give up control. They find it too scary. It's easier to give orders. An example where letting go can produce great results occurred in the steel industry. U.S. Steel and Bethlehem Steel basically didn't survive in the steel business. They explained they couldn't compete in the steel business because of their own poor workers and unfair foreign competition. Their workers weren't productive enough, and they couldn't compete with the unfair business practices that other countries were imposing upon us. Somebody forgot to tell Worthington Steel, Nucor Steel and Chaparral Steel, because they didn't accept those premises. At the same time when U.S. Steel and Bethlehem were dying, these companies were emerging. Today, these three companies have productivity levels that average over 200 percent above the international level. In other words, they are doing better than twice as good as overseas companies. Not bad for a work force that wasn't productive. The difference is that these companies are great examples of companies that have empowered their work forces from top to bottom. They ask their employees for ideas, but more importantly, they incorporate those ideas into the business plan. Their productivity has soared, because these people feel like they are a part of the company, not just pawns that are being moved around by upper management.

Wright
What can people do to become better leaders?

Mission Possible!

Garrison

The obvious answer is learning and practice. Everyone should attend seminars, read books and listen to tapes on leadership, then practice implementing what he or she has learned. Leadership is like riding a bike: You don't learn it by reading a book; you have to do it. Everyone must understand that it takes work and time to become a leader but that almost everyone has some leadership potential. Leadership needs to start by listening to customers. That doesn't mean just the external customer but also the internal customer, which is the employee. The workers face many concerns, too. When dealing with the customer, how can we solve their problems if we don't listen to them to understand their problems? When companies start assuming what other people's problems are and going off in a direction that benefits themselves, which is what many business have done in the past, those companies will have problems. This was the case with U.S. Steel's problem. They basically told the customer to do it their way or else. Unfortunately, the steel companies' customers selected "or else."

Wright

Right.

Garrison

Worthington Steel has a different philosophy. They listen to their customers and then provide what the customer wants. They also do this with their employees. Leadership is a long-term investment. It doesn't happen overnight. For this reason, companies must start training people the day they walk in the door. No one expects an army private to run the war, but they look for him to do his constantly changing job. With this approach, by the time someone is a foreman, he's learned the necessary leadership skills for that position. This approach allows people to learn the necessary skills that are appropriate to his or her level one step at a time. Since it takes time to be an experienced leader, we can't just say, "Now you're a leader; so lead."

Another thing that people need to accept is that leaders don't know or have to know all the answers. Too often, managers and CEOs can't admit that they don't know everything. They are afraid that if they admit that, they will lose control. Accept the idea that the people on the front line often have a better idea about what to do than those on the upper floors of corporate America. If you're in charge, you had better have some idea of what's going on, but you can't know every detail. If you must decide everything, you might as well get rid of everyone else since you will be doing everything anyway. The rest of the company will be just watching you. Accept that the world is changing too fast for you to control everything. If you're not out there in the field, how can you know what the customer wants right now? It's leadership's responsibility to help create a company philosophy. Companies that successfully deal with issues create a culture in their company, which is part of its governance process. Instead of rules, the company creates a culture that gives people an understanding and a feeling on how to operate.

For example, Nordstrom's has such a culture for taking care of its customers. When there is a problem, their salespeople are empowered to take care of the customer on the spot. Salespeople don't have to ask management for approval. Salespeople don't have to ask, "What should we do?" Instead, they react based upon their training. The Ritz has the same kind of attitude. Every employee can spend up to $2,000 without any approval to satisfy a customer on the spot. I'm talking about housekeepers, maintenance people, waitresses, et cetera. Yes, even entry-level people can spend up to $2,000 to take care of a customer on the spot without asking for approval or permission or asking what to do. This approach breeds leadership. This approach is critical, because by the time the question gets up to management and the response is returned, the situation has changed so that management's answer is probably wrong and at best, it's late. Usually, an adequate response provided quickly is better than a late perfect response.

When you try to encourage leadership in everyone, expect to find resistance. Why? It's harder to be a leader than it is to be a manager. It's easy to tell someone, "I want you to do this or else." It's much more difficult to tell people, "Take care of it and I'll back your decision." However, this empowers people and helps attract the best people. In the end, you obtain better results. Good people have an entrepreneurial spirit, and they want to have some say in what they are doing. They don't want to be told what to do. If we tell all the time, we will push away the good people. Of course, common sense is needed. We must make sure the person was trained for the task at hand before we delegate. A challenge is that people with an entrepreneurial spirit can be difficult to deal with.

We can go back and look at school, and I laugh at this one. I do some testing on personality traits. The people who tend to take charge and have an entrepreneurial spirit are usually heavily right-brained and enjoy challenging the status quo. I often ask the entrepreneurially-spirited people in my seminars, "How many of you spent a lot of time in the principal's office when you were growing up?" Most of them raise their hand. These people have been challenging the system and ruffling feathers for a long time. But they are successful, because they don't let obstacles get in the way. Of course, we have to keep it in perspective. We can't do things that are illegal, unethical, immoral or unsafe. Some business leaders recently seem to have forgotten this point, and we should pull the plug on them. But the real leader is not just about personal success; he or she makes his subordinates a success by encouraging their leadership. Remember, leadership is about empowering your people to go out and do things. When leaders do that, their people rally around the mission and achieve amazing results.

Wright

Are these kinds of people on their way to being leaders, or are they leaders already. Do you think leaders are born?

Garrison

While we expect to find leaders at the top of an organization—even though that's not always true—most people don't expect to find leaders at the bottom of organizations. This is a shame, because they are there. Some are just unpolished gems. They have leadership potential, and it needs to be brought out. Most people have a tremendous amount of leadership ability, but it needs be practiced and nurtured. Just like an athlete—no matter how good a natural athlete a person is—that individual will not excel unless he or she practices the sport. "Are leaders born or made?" I love to tease people who ask that question by responding, "Have you ever known a leader that wasn't born?" Of course, some people have natural leadership ability, just like some people are better athletes, but leadership is a skill that can be learned. We can all learn to be better leaders. We all need to invest time and effort at becoming better leaders, and we need to encourage everyone around us to do the same. There are a few people out there who, for whatever reason, just don't want the extra responsibility. That's fine. But the majority of people do, and we should encourage that, support that, help them in every way that we can, because we will create a much better and stronger organization.

Wright

If that's the case, then how do you develop leadership, or how do you develop leaders?

Garrison

There are a couple of ways. On an individual basis, we need to improve our communication skills, and that includes both speaking and listening. The other thing managers should be doing is loosening up. Managers are often inflexible and want to keep things under their control. Leadership is about being confident enough to let other people take or assume responsibility and even make mistakes. The big problem is that some people have authority and responsibility confused. In some organizations, senior management wants to delegate responsibility while still keeping the control and authority. Effective leadership is about keeping the responsibility and delegating the authority, because you can never delegate responsibility. Yet we see management blame the rank and file all the time for company problems.

For example, if a salesperson doesn't sell a product that doesn't work, the salesperson is often fired, because the sales goals weren't

Mission Possible!

reached. Management doesn't take responsibility for the shoddy product. For example, I was a lieutenant in the army, and I was an air defense officer. We had to train our people to pass a visual aircraft recognition exam. It's probably one of the toughest exams most people ever have to take. The test is to identify every aircraft in the world instantaneously in profile—from underneath, from a side view, from a top view, from a front view or from rear view. In a combat situation, you usually can't read the symbols on the sides, so you better know who's who. The "friendlies" do get mad when you shoot at them. For this reason, everyone in air defense is made to take a test to ensure they know their aircraft. During the exam, they flash a slide of an aircraft on the screen for a couple of seconds, and you have to write down the aircraft. The rules were simple: Everyone in a company-size unit passes or everyone fails.

I was on active duty during Vietnam, and many of our soldiers were draftees and didn't want to be there. The challenge: How do you motivate these soldiers to want to learn this material? The test had twenty slides, and you had to get fifteen correct in order to pass the test. Most officers threatened people, "If you don't pass, you will be sorry." My roommate and I tried a different approach. We each told our platoon, "I think you are smarter than my roommate's platoon. Now if you men do better on our test than they do, then the other lieutenant will buy you all the beer you can drink at a party." They thought that idea was great! Our private contest was based upon the total score for the platoon; the platoon with the highest score would win. There was a catch. If everyone but one man scored a perfect score and the other man failed, then the platoon would receive a total score of zero and lose.

The results were amazing. We had forty-two people in our two platoons take the test. Half of our men earned perfect scores. One man got three wrong, and the rest of the men either got one or two wrong. The other platoon in our battery passed, because they did something similar. However, none of the other nine platoons in the battalion passed the test. No other platoon except our two had a perfect score, yet half of our people got perfect scores.

The immediate reaction was that we cheated somehow. They took some of the privates and said they were going to retest them. They put them in the test room one at time, and when they all passed, the next question was, "How did you do it?" The difference was positive motivation. We made passing the test to be in their best interest. My roommate and I treated both platoons to a beer party. It was well worth it. We partied while the other platoons sat in classrooms learning about aircraft recognition. Our way was the better way. The results are amazing when you change it around and give people the responsibility and the authority to take care of the situation. Our men would ask for help when they needed it. We didn't make people take classes; they asked for them. Our men walked around with their little flash cards. They were quizzing each other every time they had a break. Peers made sure other platoon members knew their stuff. They wanted to make sure everyone received high scores. We empowered our platoons and achieve unbelievable results.

Wright

You talked about positive results. Let me ask you this question: What are some of the biggest mistakes that leaders make?

Garrison

I guess one of the biggest is that they fail to let go. I understand how owners of companies feel; it's their money. They remind me that since it's their money, they need to control everything. I tease them and ask, "How many people here don't make mistakes?" Nobody raises his or her hand. I then ask, "Why don't you let your people make some of their own mistakes instead of just making yours?" I do get some strange looks. But I add, "I understand that you don't send somebody out there who's untrained, unqualified to do something. You've got to use common sense here. But after you train somebody to do the job, then why don't you just let him or her do the job." It's amazing how this approach changes the dynamics.

Executives need to understand that a company is like a child. After all, it is their baby. Just a like a child, a company needs to be allowed to grow up on its own. Give it guidance, but it needs to make its

Mission Possible!

own decisions, or, in this case, employees need to make decisions. If you control every element of the company, it can't grow. You will suffocate it. You must train your people, educate your people and give them the necessary skills. Then let go!

There are only a few reasons why people are unsuccessful when they try something. One is that they are not trained. That's management's responsibility. Secondly, they don't have the abilities or don't have the information they need. That's management's responsibility. Third, they are not motivated. It's management's responsibility to create an atmosphere where they are motivated. I ask them, "What kind of attitude do employees usually have on the first day of work?" They answer, "Ah, of course, they are excited." I follow up with, "If your people are not excited every day at work, what have you done to them? They were working when they arrived, so how did you break them?" That gets some strange looks.

Another related issue is the need for excessive control or reporting. In one seminar, I was kind of kidding when I said, "Sometimes, I think we should just throw away the computers." The audience cheered, which surprised me a little. I asked them why they felt that way. I deal with construction audiences, and this group was mostly project managers, and they complained that they were spending up to two hours a day updating their schedules. Plus they had to spend additional time preparing other reports for senior management. Unfortunately, they are not paper pushers. Project managers are supposed to be building something, not writing about it. They are frustrated. The problem is that computers have made reporting easier, so the reports have grown. People need to ask, "Do I really need this report?" Too many people are wasting time writing reports that have little impact. But management tells me that the report is to make sure they are doing their jobs. Duh! If you are worried, go out and see if the building is going up instead of asking them to tell you they are building it. In the end, the reports aren't read, or upper management wastes time reading them—both lose-lose situations. We need to find ways to change our approach. We need to give people the authority and the power to go do their jobs and avoid excess control.

Another problem is that too often, people tend to hire people like themselves. Of course, it's easier. If the person thinks like me, talks like me and walks like me, I know exactly what he is going to do. But if you hire mavericks, they will keep you on your toes and might even teach you something new. Heaven forbid they have a better idea than you. That makes some people uncomfortable. Companies tell their people they must deal with change, yet often, owners or senior management are the most rigid. Owners need to adapt to the changing work environment. Leaders need to deal with change. This means listening to other perspectives and accepting other perspectives. This can be very difficult for some people. But companies will suffer when their owners and/or leaders don't adapt.

Another problem is the lack of or inability to give enough encouragement. This is a very difficult thing for a lot of people. It is difficult to say, "Hey, you've done a great job! Keep it up! I'm behind you a hundred percent." Practice saying those statements; it's really not that hard. It doesn't have to be some monumental accomplishment. A woman executive from a Fortune 500 company illustrates the point. Whenever one of her people used to do something, anything that was good, she would send them a note, an "Atta boy!" by e-mail. It simply said, "Great job. I really appreciate what you are doing with _____." Nothing complicated; just a little thank-you. She didn't think anything of it. She just assumed it was part of her job, patting her people on the back. Her people were scattered all over several states, so she couldn't walk into their offices and pat them on the back in person, so she did it by e-mail. She didn't think much of it until one day she walked in to one of those people's office. She was on the road, and she needed a pen for something. She said, "Can I borrow a pen?" The worker said, "Yeah, sure, no problem. Just help yourself. There's one in my top drawer." The executive pulled open the drawer and found a stack e-mails. The executive asked, "What are these?" She knew what they were but was curious why they were there. The worker responded, "Oh, those are all your e-mails. The first thing I do every morning when I come in is I read them."

Now can you think of a better way to start your day? When your boss says, "I think you walk on water," your boss thinks you are doing

Mission Possible!

a great job. Is there any doubt why this person keeps getting more little thank-you notes? While this is a simple story, it certainly reinforces the message. When people know you care, they try twice as hard.

Wright

Well, I think I'm beginning to find out why you are such a good speaker and teacher on the subject of leadership. Ted, I really appreciate you being with us today on *Mission Possible!* I have learned a lot. I think our readers and our listeners both will learn a lot. I appreciate your taking this time out of your schedule. I really do thank you for being with us.

Garrison

Thank you.

Wright

Today we have been talking with Ted Garrison. For over twenty-five years, he has worked in both the real estate and construction business. Most of his time now is spent on educating people on how to become better leaders. That's good for all of us. Thank you so much, Ted.

Garrison

Thank you. Take care.

Ted Garrison
Garrison Associates
1092 Hampstead Lane
Ormond Beach, Florida 32174
Phone: 386.437.6713
Fax: 386.437.9841
Mobile: 386.846.5954
Email: Growing@TedGarrison.com
www.TedGarrison.com

Chapter 11

THOMAS WINNINGER

Thomas Winninger's market strategies have been featured on CNBC and in First Business, Boardroom Reports, Venture *and* Success Magazine, *and he has been published in more than 300 other trade journals, publications and newspapers. He's frequently referred to as America's leading marketing strategist and the man who is reinventing the way America captures market share.*

The Interview

David E. Wright (Wright)

Thomas Winninger is the founder of the Winninger Institute for Marketing Strategy and the author of the best-selling books *Price Wars, Hiring Smart, Sell Easy* and the soon-to-be-released *Full Price*. He's one of the most in-demand speakers in the United States today. He and his company have received many awards and commendations, including the Blue Chip Enterprise Award from the United States Chamber of Commerce, a nomination for America's Entrepreneur of the Year award and the 1995 Cavett Award, the highest award given by the 4,000 members of the National Speakers Association. In 1987, he was inducted into the CPAE Speaker Hall of Fame. His market strategies have been featured on CNBC and in *First Business, Boardroom Reports, Venture* and *Success Magazine*, and he has been published in more than 300 other trade journals, publications and news-

Mission Possible!

lished in more than 300 other trade journals, publications and newspapers. He's frequently referred to as America's leading marketing strategist and the man who is reinventing the way America captures market share. Thom Winninger, welcome to *Mission Possible!*

Thomas Winninger (Winninger)

It's great being with you.

Wright

Thom, you're one of the country's experts on branding. According to you, Starbucks has woven coffee into the fabric the life, Harley Davidson has become a lifestyle, and Volvo is the safe car. How do you suggest that companies communicate their brands?

Winninger

It's significant today that a brand is a culture, and truly a brand is not what it is but what it does. In other words, everything you do creates some kind of branded image in the mind of your customer. If you haven't defined what your brand is, you probably have a customer that already has, and you don't even know it. Everything we do defines the brand. The way we pick up the phone, the way we communicate in our advertising, the way we respond to customers' problems. So my challenge for most organizations is take whatever you think your brand should be and define it in terms of two things: a term and a definition. For example, McDonald's would be "fast food." That's their terminology. BMW would be "riding experience." Marriott's corporate hotels would be "office away from home." I always say that Domino's Pizza's is home delivery, not the pizza itself. The minute you come up with the term, you then look for a definition that supports it. In everything we do, we should be more focused on how we define our brand in terms of experience and also ask if there is a gap between that definition and what the customer thinks our definition is. So today's customer might say that McDonald's is slow food, not fast food. That's not necessarily what it is, but sometimes, and in many cases, these gaps do exist.

Wright

Price doesn't seem to matter at Starbucks either. I know the coffee is great. Even when I go into Barnes and Noble or one of these places, I pay exorbitant fees for coffee, just because it's an experience.

Winninger

Right. Barnes and Noble today is not a place where you buy a book. It's a place where you buy a cup of coffee and then read a book that you put back on the shelf, because there's more profitability in the coffee than there might be in the book.

Wright

You teach companies to make their brands a celebrity and create brand loyalty. What are some of the methods you use?

Winninger

I always say that celebrity status is created, because there's a uniqueness that makes you stand out in a crowd. So celebrity tends to mean differentiation. It goes back to what I asked in the first response: What is the differentiation that makes you stand out, and how do you play that out? In other words, if you want to be a celebrity, you have to be what you say you are, and you have to be visible—highly visible—in front of customers who want to be attracted to that uniqueness. It's the magic of three. But that really isn't my idea. The magic of three came from the book *Life is a Contact Sport* by Ken Kragen, who was Kenny Rogers's manager. He always said, "If you really want to be a celebrity, it's the magic of three." In other words, you want to make sure that three things happen together. When Kenny Rogers was hitting Las Vegas, he had received a Grammy the week before, and his movie was coming out the week after. Vertical contact, or vertical visibility, around actions tends to heighten celebrity status. If I'm speaking in Toronto to a given group, and the Toronto newspaper features an article on me the week before, and a radio station does an interview with me that day, and then I speak, there's more chance that there will be a celebrity status related to me in Toronto.

Mission Possible!

Every business must think about this. For example, let's say a salesperson makes a call, doesn't sell what he has to offer but writes a thank-you note after it's over. Then if he sends the prospective customer an article related to something he wrote about that appears to be in print, there tends to be a heightened sense of importance, i.e., differentiation, i.e., celebrity status. I always say that celebrities aren't always the best at what they do, but they're most visible at what they do, and that creates celebrity status. Any business can do this with its brand.

Wright

And that creates loyalty? Are people loyal to celebrity status?

Winninger

People tend to be loyalty to "the truth." In other words, people tend to be loyal to things that are what they believe they are. So if I believe that Disney is family entertainment, and that's what I want, then I'm loyal to them. If I believe that you're a car company or dealership, and you give the best service in town, then I'm going to be loyal to you, because loyalty tends to come from structured consistency and truth. So if you are what you say you are, I tend to be more loyal to you. Do you see where I'm going with that? If I go to see Bruce Springsteen, and he is what I think he is, that's truth. As a result of that, I say, "Wow, Bruce Springsteen. I'll go see him anywhere I can." That's truth. That's loyalty. That's celebrity status.

Wright

Thom, I would like to quote you. In reading some of your material, I found something you said that really interested me. "Everyone from accounting firms to sneaker makers to restaurants is trying to figure out how to transcend their category and create buzz like Hilfiger." Is that really possible for most companies?

Winninger

The leadership companies in most categories have created buzz. Is it possible for everybody? Yes, as long as you can find a tipping point or a point of differentiation. The minute you can find a point of differentiation, you can create buzz. Tommy Hilfiger is style, along with that logo look that he's created with the red and blue and white. He can put that anywhere today, whether the Hilfiger name is on it or not, and people will know what it is. So I would say yes. Buzz for him is a look that was different than everybody else's. Then, interestingly enough, he didn't just take the look but he built a concept around it that sustained the buzz. He built a department that the store could install that became the Tommy Hilfiger signature department. It just continues to perpetuate itself. Buzz is a tipping point, or differentiation, a sustainable communication of that in the marketplace and a uniqueness that tends to keep people talking. By nature, buzz is your ability to do things that tend to create that conversation. In other words, are you where it's happening? Are you visible where it's happening?

I've got a friend here in Minneapolis named Wayne Kostroski. He owns several restaurants, and he also is the founder of Taste of NFL. He puts on a multimillion-dollar fundraiser at the beginning of the Super Bowl games, in which the coach from each of the NFL teams sponsors a chef. He spends the whole year creating buzz around that event, putting out press releases, being visible at the right places, using the endorsements of the celebrity chefs, getting endorsements from the coaches and each of these NFL communities, tying in to a concierge service. That connection tends to proliferate the buzz. Buzz is consistency of communication. I always say that if you're not visible to a customer six times a year, you're not even creating minimum buzz.

Wright

I was fascinated by one of your topics, *Market Quake 2010*, in which you say that seventy-eight percent of America's organizations will have to reinvent the way they do business in the next eight years. Could you tell us what you mean?

Winninger

Yes. Seventy-eight percent of America's businesses are living off an old paradigm and an old customer definition. As a result of that, they tend to look at the universe of their customer, not the profile of their customer. For example, a business could say, "Gee, I'm a grocery store. There are 10,000 people coming through my front door this week. I've got 10,000 customers." But instead, they should be ferreting out which types of customers best meet the profile they seek to serve and which of those types are creating the demand or are the dominant paradigm or profile of the future. In a grocery store, for example, the profile customer of today is "take home a meal." How many of the 10,000 customers in your store are take-home-a-meal customers, and is your store profiled as a take-home-a-meal store? If you're there, then you have already started the process of defining yourself and reinventing yourself for the future.

I'm saying this hypothetically, but let's say that Marriott Hotels looks at everybody who stays at a Marriott as a guest. My question is, though, who is the profiled guest? If we were going to appear unique to a profile that needs us consistently and be willing to pay added dollars for value and be the dominant value to that profile of customer for the future, what are those customers going to demand of us? They're going to demand a communication port in every room. They're going to demand a laptop, or at least laptop-accessible technology in every room. They're going to find a way to stay at the hotel without having to check in. And they're going to want a continued response to make sure that at any given hotel they get first choice of which room is best for them. I question whether the hotel industry—not to point a finger at Marriott—is doing that today. They might say they are. If they are, then they're taking a step toward the solution of reinventing themselves. A company's failure today is a failure of profiling the changing dominant customer profile of tomorrow, and seventy-eight percent of the companies in America have not done that yet.

Wright

So they're going to have to find out not only who their customer is but what kind of person. Coming up with a profile is almost like niche marketing, isn't it?

Winninger

Exactly—from a customer's standpoint, not from a product standpoint. In other words, in strategy, we ask, "Do you want a great product looking for a unique customer, or do you want a unique customer looking for a great product?" I would prefer to have the customer. I would prefer to know the customer almost better than I know my product, because my product is always, in this kind of economy and marketplace, evolving to a higher level of application. If I'm capable of profiling the customer's changing need, I probably have a better shot at being the leader in providing that in the future.

Wright

One of the old paradigms is that availability creates demand. You're actually saying the opposite: Find out who the customer is, and see what he wants.

Winninger

That's right, because availability today will do nothing but confuse today's changing customer, and that's because today's changing customer technically wants greater variety and less choice. Now that's a very confusing thing, but let's say that I walk into a grocery store, and there are 40,000 SKUs—40,000 different items on the shelves in that grocery store. I'm going to walk out with 150. I've got to find my 150, and you make it tougher and tougher every year, Mr. and Mrs. Grocer. Most businesses tend to do that. They tend to bombard the customer with variety and selection and make it tougher to make a choice, because they don't understand the customer. Or they're trying to serve a universe that is too large, because they think everybody could be their customers.

Wright

I was interested in your presentation entitled *Price Wars*. You said that the one closest to the customer doesn't have to compete. What do you mean by "the closest"?

Winninger

It refers to what I said in the previous question: Those who know the changing profile of the customer are in a leadership position and do not have to compete. If they're competing with anybody, they're competing with their own ability to deliver at the customer's demand level. The research we have done says that the customer shops the Internet but buys direct. Shops the Internet, buys direct. That goes back to a percentage figure we came up with a number of years ago that says fifty-six percent of today's consumers pretty much don't know how to buy. In other words, fifty-six percent of today's consumers want to be educated before they make a decision, so they use the Internet for the access to the information, to get educated, and then they go direct to buy.

Yesterday, I was meeting with a company that's in the mortgage business, a dot-com place where people can actually apply for a loan. They said it's fascinating to them how very few people actually secure a loan on a dot-com or Web site. Rather, they use it to access the information and then go to the company directly, because they also offer face-to-face, on-site loan application. Be careful of how you're using the Internet, because it might very well destroy you if you're trying to become an Internet competitor for transactions rather than information and communication. On the other hand, the lead dog has the better view. In other words, if Hertz knows the business traveler better than any other car company, technically, they don't have to compete, because what they're doing is supplying the customer's highest need. I remember Ray Kroc asking this years ago: "Who is the best customer, and what is their highest need?" At that point, research showed that the best customer for McDonald's was in a van with a couple of kids in the back at the drive-through. If they knew that customer very, very well, why would they be watching any other fast-food format? They need to make sure that what they're delivering to that customer is satisfying. What they want those kids to have—and at that point it was a Happy Meal—was a toy, a drink, and don't eat the food. That's where they were going, closest to the customer.

Wright

You suggest forming strategic alliances to better capture the market. Could you elaborate on how this is done?

Winninger

It comes from the trend that a customer wants—a supply point. In other words, today's busy, changing consumer profile says, "I don't want to have to go to four stores to get a computer and software; I want to go to a source. So the source is the buying paradigm today. So if you are not the source, but a component of the source, you should figure out a way to create strategic alliances so that consumers view you as the source.

For example, if you're a contractor or a remodeler putting an extra bedroom on a home, you probably ought to handle everything, including the floor coverings and landscaping so that the customer sees it as turnkey, so he doesn't have to go to five sources to finish the job. Strategic alliances would tie you into a decorator, a landscaper and a floor covering operation to make sure that the customer sees you as the source. A big trend in the marketplace today is what we call "backyard entertainment." It's phenomenal as an emerging trend. It says, as Faith Popcorn did in her book, that there's a whole component of cocooning going on in the marketplace, which means that customers don't want to go out—they want to go home. At home, they want to have things that make them feel like they're out. In other words, if I go to a restaurant, sit outside and they have heaters, I want a heater on my patio. If I sit by a fireplace at a restaurant, I want a fireplace on my patio. If I want to hear a waterfall, I want a waterfall on my patio. If I'm a landscaper facing this marketplace, I'll probably tie into a patio/casual furniture store, I'll tie into a hearth store, I'll tie into an outdoor kitchen designer, and I become vertically integrated. Even though I might not own any of those businesses, we work together to ensure that the strategic alliance creates a seamless source for the customer.

I'll give you the question for your customer: What can we be doing for you that you're doing for yourself or having someone else do related to our product and service? Identify what these are, and then

Mission Possible!

build strategic alliances around them. Not to elongate the answer, but we must understand that the culture and the quality of service delivered by one business must be equal to the quality of service delivered by all to make it a true, seamless, strategic alliance.

Wright

So it does matter whom you form an alliance with?

Winninger

As long as the quality of service and the culture are the same. So if I do a great job, and the landscaper does a lousy job, and the casual furniture place does a marginal job, we will never be seen as a single-source supply unit. The service dynamic must be similar. So the car dealership sells you the car and then calls you on the phone, picks up the car, changes the oil and keeps the car serviced so you don't go to Jiffy Lube—and there's nothing wrong with a Jiffy Lube—but I'd say that if I had the responsibility of selling cars, I'd make sure that I closed the loop with someone who could service the car so that customers could see us as a total-source supply.

Wright

Thom, with our *Mission Possible!* talk show and book we're trying to encourage people in our audience to live better and be more fulfilled by listening to the examples of our guests. Is there anything or anyone in your life who has made a difference for you and helped you to become a better person?

Winninger

I do believe that all of us need some kind of friend or mentor to challenge us with commitments that pull us through to completion. My best friend, Dan, and I have monthly meetings, at which he challenges me to work on different components of my life over the course of the next month. I have found in my personal life—if that's what you happen to be relating to—that balance is the key. When any one component of my personal life gets out of balance, it seems like the wheels are coming off. So if I'm spending too much time civically, and I'm not doing projects with the kids—we have four under the age of seventeen—there's an imbalance. So I came up with different theme areas, and I apply one to each month, which focuses me on that component of my personal and business life.

For example, one theme might be to focus more on the success of my people each day. So each day, I make sure that one of my associates gets a compliment from me or reinforcement from me, and I work on that for a month. What I've typically found is that if you do that thing for a month, it becomes more automatic for you, and you don't need to spend that much focus time on it. So the next month, I focus on identifying the things that create summit outcomes for me. In other words, of the twenty things I have to do today, what are the three that will get me the most outcome for the input? And I focus on that for a month, and I do the same thing in my personal life.

Wright

So you're forming habits?

Winninger

Correct. And I do that Dan's help. Now we only get together for coffee once a month, so it's not a serious mentor/protégé relationship. But we all need to do that for each other. The best reflection in a life is a friend's feedback.

Wright

What do you think makes a great mentor? In other words, are there characteristics that great mentors have in common?

Winninger

I think number one is the ability to ask questions that challenge us to commit to action. Number two is not upstaging the protégé with what you're doing as a mentor. I think role modeling is one thing, but if somebody says, "This is what I'm working on" and the other person is constantly saying, "Well, this is what I did," then you're trying to make the protégé do what you've done rather than lift him to the outcome of his own skills. The protégé has within him or her what it takes to be successful. The mentor's challenge is to draw the focus of the person to what he can do that makes him a hare, not a tortoise.

I've always had a problem with the fact that the tortoise won the race and the hare lost. We all try to model the tortoise. We're all saying, "Be like me. Be methodical. Plod along, and somebody will make a mistake, and you'll be alright." But I don't want to spend my life waiting for somebody else to make a mistake. I would prefer to look within myself, look at my talents, skills, environment and the commitment I've made and see how I can capitalize on running that race in a way that's best for me.

Wright

I was talking to a good friend of yours, Jim Cathcart, the other day. We were talking about mentors who really didn't know that they were mentors, and Jim told me that Bill Gove had died recently, which I didn't know. That man will never know how much impact he had on my life in my early years. I remember growing up listening to every single word that Bill said.

Winninger

Isn't that interesting? I always felt that some people are silent mentors, and I think you hit on it. My challenge to people is, at some time in your life, to drop a card or a note to your silent mentor, saying "I've admired you for years, and you've made a difference in my life without knowing it. Thanks." It would be fascinating how many of these we probably could write. You know the old saying—the teacher is there when the student is ready? I think each mentor plays a different role in a different component, and that's unique. Bill Gove is definitely, for many of us, the silent mentor, and he wasn't very silent!

Wright

Most people are fascinated with these new television shows about being a survivor. What has been the greatest comeback that you have made from adversity in your career or in your life?

Winninger

In my business, I had channeled myself into a category that was eliminated within eighteen months. In the early '80s I had specialized in construction real estate, because that was my family's business, and interest rates had gone up to eighteen percent. The market evaporated in a very short period of time. The opportunities to speak, the opportunities to consult and strategize for clients went away, because many of the clients went away. In the midst of that I had met Nito Cobain, who said, "Why don't you come and visit me, and let's talk about this?" When Nito got done asking me questions, he said, "It's interesting, Thom, that the material that you brought to the construction real estate market is superior and leverageable." I said, "What does that mean?" He said, "The concepts cross industry lines. What I'd like you to do is challenge yourself to go back through all your material and pick out the things from different industries that you believe would relate to those industries." In less than a month, Nito had either given me the skill or challenged me to develop the skill of seeing the strategic imperatives of many different industries. Today, I have applied those to more than twenty-four different industries that all think that they're unique to them. That was a real turnaround for me, and in fewer than twenty-four months, we were back to where we were before. In forty-eight months, we had almost doubled what we did in the real estate construction arena, and I've stayed with that all along.

Wright

What impresses me so much about Nito Cobain is that he's very philanthropic. He has foundations, and he does all kinds of things that give back to the community. I've gained a new respect for him.

Winninger

Absolutely. It's interesting to me not only that Nito gives at a tremendous level himself but that he has the ability to draw other people into the commitment. And I think that's truly what a philanthropic person is all about, being a great role model for other people.

Wright

When you consider the choices that you've made through the years, has faith played an important role in your life?

Winninger

Truly. I'm a faith-based person. We call ourselves "cradle Catholics." I'm a product of a Jesuit education, and Ignatius Loyola founded the Jesuits on faith-based decision making, or discernment. It was a process he wrote a book about four or five hundred years ago, but it is still relevant today. I have based my business decisions on his process of discernment, which ties in faith as a unique component. It's a wonderful process. I would challenge anybody to look up Ignatius Loyola. It's an easy read.

Wright

If you could tell our audience and readers something that you feel would help them or encourage them, what would you say?

Winninger

I would say that I have never met a person who made a commitment to be unique who ended up as a failure. A person who makes a decision to be unique and then operates based upon that commitment has never been a failure. If anybody finds such a person, I'd like to know who it is. Once you make the decision to be unique, you identify those things that are important to the people around you—be they clients, customers, family, children, whatever—and you become successful. The people who make the decision to do a lot of things oftentimes fail. I think that if I could share that as part of my life passion or mission, I would be very gratified when I look back and wonder how I have helped people. So in your marriage or in your relationship with a significant other, how can you be different to the point of the other person's satisfaction? Can you call her voice mail and leave a message, "I was thinking about you today, and I really appreciate what you did last night"? That makes you different. Can you write a card and tack it on the mirror before you take a trip? Can you pick out something small and inexpensive—but something that shows that you think about that person—and acquire it for her? It makes you different. I know you can apply that same personal principle to your clients. But seeking to be different in life in terms of other people's needs tends to make you successful over the long haul. It's not just about doing more. Don't tell me how much you've gotten done. Don't tell me how many club presidencies you had. Tell me what you did as club president that created a significant turn and was unique to your members.

Wright

That's great advice. This half hour has just zipped by, and we are at the end of it. I really do appreciate you being a guest on *Mission Possible!* today, Thom. Thom Winninger is the founder of the Winninger Institute for Marketing Strategy. Among his many awards is the Cavett Award, which is the Oscar of the speaking industry. We really appreciate the information that you've given us today, and we appreciate your being a guest on *Mission Possible!*

Winninger

Thank you very much. It's been my honor.

Winninger Institute
3300 Edinborough Way, Suite 701
Minneapolis, Minnesota 55435
Phone: 952.896.1900
Fax: 952.896.9784
Email: Thomas@winninger.com
www.winninger.com

Chapter 12

DONALD L. RHEEM

Donald L. Rheem is an award winning former White House correspondent and Washington, D.C. Bureau Chief, and Cabinet-level speechwriter who is now one of the nation's leading media trainers and personal communication coaches. His clients include corporate executives, U.S. Senators, even royalty. He also serves as an advisor on marketing, public relations, and crisis communications to clients nationwide. You have seen his clients on every major television network, in virtually every newspaper and national news magazine.

The Interview

David E. Wright (Wright)

Today, we're talking with Donald L. Rheem. Mr. Rheem is an award-winning, former print and broadcast journalist, Washington, D.C., bureau chief, cabinet-level speech writer and White House correspondent. He is also one of the nation's leading media trainers and personal communication coaches. His clients include corporate executives, U.S. senators, federal government entities and royalty. He also serves as an advisor to organizations around the country on marketing, public relations and crisis communications. You have seen his clients on every major television network and in virtually every newspaper and national magazine. Don began his Washington career as a consultant to the Science Committee in the U.S. House of Representatives, which was followed by several years as an advisor to the Secretary of Health and Human Services. Donald Rheem, welcome to *Mission Possible!*

Donald L. Rheem (Rheem)
David, it's a pleasure to be here, talking about how people can become more successful by simply improving their communication skills.

Wright
What is the linkage between success and communication? It seems that some people are just born good speakers. They love an audience and never get nervous.

Rheem
Well, it is true that some people just seem to be natural speakers. They're not afraid of an audience, and they just get right up front and start talking. Some of them don't even need a script. They can just get up and talk extemporaneously. Those are some of the best and most fun speakers to listen to, because they are unscripted and tend to have a lot more vitality, energy and variety in what they say. However, for most of us, there is a bit of nervousness associated with public speaking, and that is okay. A little nervous energy can help to keep us focused.

Going back to the linkage between success and communication, it's pretty clear that the way we communicate, both verbally and with our body language, is one of the most critical factors in how people assess us, how they rank us and how they decide they are going to relate to us. There have been a number of studies about audiences and what they want from a speaker. They make their decisions early, from the first moments they see or meet someone, and those first impressions are critical to how they will listen and respond. People who master just a few communication skills pave the way for their own success. If we want people to listen to us, if we want to be persuasive and motivate an audience, and if we want to lead and manage well, we need to be good communicators.

Wright

So what can the rest of us do?

Rheem

If we're not born good speakers or born orators, the best way to approach it, so that we don't get overwhelmed, is simply to pick one skill at a time. Just work on one technique at a time and integrate that into our speaking style. Let's say that we're going to work on movement in the next presentation—a strategic movement such as how we approach an audience—and focus on how we use movement to exemplify what we're saying and to make a point. Just work on that one skill in the next speaking engagement, presentation, sales or marketing presentation. Then build on that, and integrate more skills into what you do.

Wright

I know there must be many great characteristics of a great speaker, but would you give our readers three of the most critical characteristics of a great speaker?

Rheem

I'm going to do this, not based on my opinion but on what some of these studies tell us about audiences and what they want. Probably one of the most important factors is to have fun. That is, your audience needs to have fun in whatever kind of a speaking environment that they're in. They want to enjoy the learning. They want to enjoy the speaker. They want that speaker to welcome them and to be friendly and humorous. That doesn't mean that you have to tell jokes, but you can't take yourself too seriously. A funny story is much less risky than a joke. Audiences definitely want to have fun.

Secondly, they need to be focused. Here is why: It isn't because audiences like crisp speakers, it's because of the way people learn. The brain needs to be able to easily organize the information that's coming in if it's going to remember it. So we need to be focused on just a few points, preferably three primary points, to make in any presentation. Stick to those three, and build examples around them, but stay focused. One of the things that audiences want to do is share what they've learned with others. The best way for us to do that is to organize the material in a way that's easy to remember.

Now my third point is that you need to find your audience before you start speaking. What I mean by that is that you need to understand that audience. You need to have done some research about them. Why are they there? How do they get ahead in life? How do they get promoted? How do they get noticed in the workplace? What are their biggest concerns right now? You need to be able to identify those things about an audience and speak to them. No matter what your material is, speak to those issues, and your audience will be receptive.

So let me just sum up. We need to have fun. We need to be focused. And we need to find that audience before we start speaking.

Wright

You work with senators, CEOs and other VIP clients. These are people who communicate all the time. Why do they come to you?

Rheem

That's a question that I asked myself when I was first began working on Capitol Hill. They speak all the time—sometimes giving two or three speeches a day to various constituencies. But here's what it boils down to: No matter how often you speak, there are things that you can do better. They understand and value that. Whether it's improving the texture of their delivery or their voice tone or simply trying to become more engaging or energetic, people can get better with coaching and practice. I also work with one of the best speech therapists in the country on the physical mechanics of speaking. How are they breathing? How are they projecting? Are they speaking from their throat or from their diaphragm? These are issues that are very important to improving the quality and energy of the way we deliver information.

Wright

There are a lot of people in this field. How do you distinguish your practice from the others?

Rheem

It's true; there are a lot of people who are communications consultants. I try to distinguish my practice by focusing on research. I've reviewed a lot of the research in adult learning and human memory so that my clients can better understand how people learn. When we're communicating, many consultants in this field simply talk about projecting and voice and body and don't focus on the audience—the people who are listening. If we understand better how people learn and what they want from a speaker and then integrate that into our material, we'll be much more successful. And that's what my clients have found over the years. I also have to say that the years I spent as a television correspondent in Washington, D.C., conducting hundreds of interviews with corporate CEOs, government officials and other dignitaries, has played a role in my practice.

Wright

If there were just one thing that you could suggest readers focus on to improve their communication skills, what would that be?

Rheem

I think I would suggest exploring the art of storytelling. There are a number of good books out there, such as Stephen Denning's The Springboard: How Storytelling Ignites Action in Knowledge-Era Organizations. The value of storytelling as an effective communication medium, even in business and professional settings, is becoming more widely recognized. Even the Harvard Business Review ran an article on storytelling recently.

Why is storytelling so effective? Because long before there was a written language or the printing press—for tens of thousands of years—Homo sapiens was communicating through storytelling. It's almost genetically encoded in us. We love stories. Just the simple technique of talking to an audience, pausing and saying, "Let me tell you a story," and then going in to make a point using an example or some other illustration, is a marvelous technique to use. It relaxes them, opens them up and makes them more receptive.

Wright

When I think about the Bible and all the literature that's in it, the bottom line is that about the only thing I remember is the stories.

Rheem

Absolutely. It's also important to remember, at least according to Bible scholars, that many of the books in the Bible were communicated by word of mouth for decades before they were ever written down. So that literature is rich with storytelling, because that's how it was preserved and handed down from one generation to the next and from one village to another.

Wright

You were a television reporter and White House correspondent. What did that teach you about personal communication?

Rheem

It was a great experience, traveling around the country interviewing people to understand their stories and then turn around and tell that story to another audience—television viewers. But I learned as a reporter that the most important thing for a person to have is a set of key messages, some focus that he or she sticks to. People would do an interview with me, and we might talk for an hour. They would answer every question I gave them. Then at the end of the interview, I would have pages of notes, but they would often say, "I never got to the points I really wanted to convey."

Speakers need to have their key points well established before they speak and then stick to them. Steer questions back to your main points. When you are finished talking, your audience should be able to easily state the three key points you were trying to make. If they can't, you have failed as a good communicator. Another point I would highlight, which actually comes from the television news business, is "Leave them wanting more." In other words, don't try to say everything you know. Tease people with just the essentials. Let them come back to you for more.

Wright

When I look at television reporters now, I often wonder how much the reporter is following his or her agenda. Does that happen in television reporting now?

Rheem

Oh, absolutely. In the business we call it "taking a voice." You often see reporters taking a voice in their coverage. We're even at a point now in television news journalism where reporters are also commentators. They're giving their opinions along with their reporting of the news. I think it's a serious problem in journalism today, this blending of opinion and news delivery. I think it's harder and harder for audiences to distinguish between what is objective news and what is simply one reporter's opinion.

Wright

It's a little scary, isn't it?

Rheem

It is scary, and there have been many seminars around the country on what is objectivity and balance in reporting. One of the things that we're asking a reporter to do is go out and look at a lot of information and then give us just the most important points. Even that act is somewhat subjective. There are some reporters who seem more dedicated to objectivity and fairness and balance than others.

Wright

You mentioned seminars. As I understand it, you give seminars all over the country, helping professionals improve their presentation and speaking skills.

What do you see as some of the greatest challenges facing speakers today?

Rheem

I would come back to the three things that I mentioned earlier. One challenge is not knowing their audience. Another is when a speaker is not having much fun or being much fun in the delivery. The third challenge would be not having a clear focus.

But I'll tell you, secondary to those three key things, one of the biggest challenges facing people making presentations today is the misuse of Microsoft PowerPoint. I am referring to an over-reliance on projection technology in order to convey information. PowerPoint is a fantastic piece of software, but it needs to be used in specific ways. Too often, it is used simply as a word processor rather a means to more easily convey visual information like photographs, charts and graphs.

Wright

I'm glad you said that. I thought maybe I was nuts. I've been booking speakers for fourteen years now, and I almost go into a panic when they bring the PowerPoint with them.

Rheem

Let me go over a couple of the key problems with that. Number one, when a speaker is delivering his remarks to the audience, he is the primary source of energy and excitement in that presentation. I always tell my clients that an audience's energy level will never exceed their own. So what happens when we rely on PowerPoint? The first thing that often happens is we have to turn the lights down so that people can see the screen well. Well what has Homo sapiens done for the last 30,000 years when it got dark?

Wright

I sleep.

Rheem

They've gone to sleep. There's a genetically encoded signal to sleep. The other thing that often happens to the speaker, the primary energy source in the room, is that he or she disappears into the shadows. We diminish our presence and impact.

The third critical mistake is putting black text on a white background. The problem with that is that the vast majority of everything that we human beings commit to memory is a visual image. It's not text; it's pictures. So here we go before our audience, turning the lights down—telling everyone to go to sleep—and then we fall into the shadows and put up a text-filled screen representing only a small portion of what people will remember at the end of the day. Those are serious problems. PowerPoint was meant to help us convey visual images, but too many presenters are using it as a word processor.

Wright

What is the best way to bring an audience to the same place so that they are all with us? Why is that important?

Rheem

One of the most challenging things about an audience is getting it to "yes" about us as a speaker and about our topic. That refers to its willingness to sit and listen. One of the easiest ways to get an audience to the same place is to use a technique I call Altitude Speaking™. I use the metaphor of altitude to help speakers and presenters to better understand how to bring an audience to a single location. It turns out that the higher the altitude at which we initially try to reach that audience, the easier it is to get them to "yes." Now, what do I mean by "high altitude"? When you're flying at 30,000 feet and you look down, you have a very broad view of the horizon, but you have very few details. When you're flying at 500 feet, you have lots of detail, the atmosphere is very dense, and there's lots of detail. You can see everything on the ground. At high altitude, we're talking about concepts, ideals, values, ideas, mission statements and vision statements. So it's always easier to open with an audience at an altitude where they can all agree. If we climb to a high enough altitude, we can find a concept or a value that we all agree on. Start with that and then move down from there.

Wright

You know, understanding and connecting with an audience is important. What are some of the techniques that you use to accomplish that?

Rheem

We spoke earlier about finding the audience and how important it is. I do a simple little exercise at the beginning of my seminars to help speakers better understand an audience. We simply look at what motivates that audience, good and bad. What moves them in their lives and careers? We talk about an audience and list all the things that are important to them. Then we do the same thing about us as a speaker—all the reasons why we're speaking and what we're trying to convey. Then I ask my clients to look at those two lists, because the one list, our list, is why we're speaking. The other list is why that audience is listening. The more synergy there is between those two lists, the more effective the speaker. We focus ninety to ninety-five percent of our energy on what we want to say and very little, if any, energy on what that audience wants and needs to hear in order for our information to be useful to them.

Wright

What about practice? What do you think about practice?

Rheem

The importance of rehearsing our remarks is critical to the success of what we do. For those of us who are not naturally born speakers, we need to get our material, master it, and then we need to rehearse it, even if it's just to the mirror. It's always better to practice in front of an audience, and when working with high-level VIPs in Washington, I've found that many of them like to do at least one dry run in an environment similar to the actual venue. When they're about to do an interview with a reporter or give a major speech, they typically rehearse with staff first. Staff members play the role of a reporter or audience members, and they rehearse that so that when that VIP goes out to deliver those remarks, it's not the first time, and it feels more comfortable. Communication is always easier, better, smoother and more natural when it's been rehearsed.

Wright

I've always thought that, even in his latter years, Art Linkletter was a good communicator. I was fortunate enough many years ago to see him make some commercials at a TV station. When you do a thirty-second commercial, it's really a little less than thirty seconds because of the in time and out time. But for about fifteen or twenty minutes, he would do these thirty-second commercials without any script, and he would stop on the dime every time. It was like an internal clock. The only way I could figure he did that was through practice.

Rheem

I was a radio deejay at an earlier point in my life, and boy, you had to know exactly how much lead time you had before a singer started to sing. You could talk over the instrumental, but you better not be talking when someone starts singing. You would have to get that down and just understand it. How many words can I get in? I've got two seconds left; how many words can I speak? Professionals like Art Linkletter and others can just get it down, and they just nail it. But they've done so many of them—hundreds of them. They just have an internal clock.

Wright

Most of us were told at some point growing up that it's not what you say but how you say it. Is that really true?

Rheem

You know, it's interesting. Most of us have heard that in some fashion. It probably seemed to us that it was a little ridiculous that what you say is not important, but here's what we found out through studies. The research indicates that this old adage turns out to be literally true. That is, the words we use have to be accurate, and the content of the message has to be meaningful and accurate. But if our voice tone and our body language do not support and concur with the words that we've chosen—that is, if there is a distinction or a dichotomy between the words that we're speaking and the way we're saying them—most people, even children, will believe the voice tone and body language to be the more accurate assessment of what the person really means and how he really feels. If we speak in a monotone and say how excited and pleased we are, and if we don't look at the audience or appear to be excited at all—in fact, if we're looking at the ceiling or the floor—people will know we're lying. That's why it's so important that once we've decided what we're going to say, we need to say it in a way that supports our words.

Wright

Donald, you've been so successful for many years. Now you're doing workshops and teaching people how to communicate. What's in it for you? I know people don't do things for the money. What do you get out of this?

Rheem

I love seeing people discover little epiphanies in the way they communicate. I love seeing them reach a new level of effectiveness. You know, there are few things in life where, when we can help people improve certain characteristics, it has an almost ubiquitous impact on what they do from that point forward. When we improve our communication skills, we're not just improving the way we address this audience or that audience but everyone. We become clearer, more concise, more effective communicators at home, at school, in the workplace and with our friends. It also can have a tremendous impact on the way people perceive us as individuals. If we're a better communicator, they perceive us as being more successful. I just love helping people find that in themselves. It's a real joy.

Wright

So according to that definition, I can become a better father, husband and citizen?

Rheem

Oh, absolutely. I was doing a presentation for the CEO of a well-known computer software company. We were in the middle of a discussion on techniques of how to be a more effective speaker, when all of a sudden, he jumped out of his chair and said, "That's it! That's exactly what I'm looking for." I asked him what he was referring to. He said, "I've been having some real challenges at home with my teenage son, and you've just given me the way to respond to him and deal with him in a more effective way." So that CEO saw the connection immediately and in a very real sense. Most of my clients find that they use the techniques in all aspects of their lives, especially because we also get into techniques on how to answer questions and deal with people who are hostile or unhappy. Those techniques seem to come in very, very handy.

Wright

If one of those guys from *60 Minutes* flies a helicopter in and sticks a microphone in my face, I guess the next thing you say determines the rest of your life in some cases.

Rheem

It certainly can. If it's any kind of a news magazine show or an investigative reporter, as soon as they start asking questions, you definitely have to be "on message." It's pretty clear that the news media often arrive with their own agenda, and we need to be very careful. There's a lot at stake when communicating to a broad audience like that.

Wright

What an interesting conversation. I've learned a lot today, and I really do appreciate the time that you've taken with me today to answer all of these questions.

Rheem

It's certainly my pleasure. I love my work, and I'm always happy to talk about it and help people see a new way to communicate. I appreciate your time and your energy in the interview.

Wright

Thank you. We've been talking today with Donald L. Rheem, an award-winning former print and broadcast journalist, Washington, D.C., bureau chief, cabinet-level speech writer and White House correspondent. As we have learned today, his expertise in effective communication skills can benefit us all. Thank you so much, Donald, for being with us.

Rheem

Thank you.

Donald L. Rheem
Rheem Media
8732 Preston Place
Chevy Chase, Maryland 20815
Phone: 301.718.4344
Email: info@RheemMedia.com
www.RheemMedia.com